African S

History, Politics, Econo

Edited by
Molefi Asante
Temple University

A Routledge Series

African Studies
History, Politics, Economics, and Culture
Molefi Asante, *General Editor*

Kwame Nkrumah's Contribution to Pan-Africanism
An Afrocentric Analysis
D. Zizwe Poe

Nyansapo (The Wisdom Knot)
Toward an African Philosophy of Education
Kwadwo A. Okrah

The Athens of West Africa
A History of International Education at Fourah Bay College, Freetown, Sierra Leone
Daniel J. Paracka, Jr.

The Yorùbá Traditional Healers of Nigeria
Mary Olufunmilayo Adekson

The 'Civil Society' Problematique
Deconstructing Civility and Southern Nigeria's Ethnic Radicalization
Adedayo Oluwakayode Adekson

Maat, the Moral Ideal in Ancient Egypt
A Study in Classical African Ethics
Maulana Karenga

Igbo Women and Economic Transformation in Southeastern Nigeria, 1900–1960
Gloria Chuku

Kwame Nkrumah's Politico-Cultural Thought and Policies
An African-Centered Paradigm for the Second Phase of the African Revolution
Kwame Botwe-Asamoah

Non-Traditional Occupations, Empowerment and Women
A Case of Togolese Women
Ayélé Léa Adubra

Contending Political Paradigms in Africa
Rationality and the Politics of Democratization in Kenya and Zambia
Shadrack Wanjala Nasong'o

Law, Morality and International Armed Intervention
The United Nations and ECOWAS in Liberia
Mourtada Déme

The Hidden Debate
The Truth Revealed about the Battle over Affirmative Action in South Africa and the United States
Akil Kokayi Khalfani

Britain, Leftist Nationalists and the Transfer of Power in Nigeria, 1945–1965
Hakeem Ibikunle Tijani

Western-Educated Elites in Kenya, 1900–1963
The African American Factor
Jim C. Harper, II

Africa and IMF Conditionality
The Unevenness of Compliance, 1983–2000
Kwame Akonor

Africa and IMF Conditionality

The Unevenness of Compliance, 1983–2000

Kwame Akonor

Routledge
Taylor & Francis Group
LONDON AND NEW YORK

Routledge
Taylor & Francis Group
711 Third Avenue,
New York, NY 10017

Routledge
Taylor & Francis Group
2 Park Square
Milton Park, Abingdon
Oxon OX14 4RN

Routledge is an imprint of Taylor & Francis Group, an Informa business

First issued in paperback 2012

International Standard Book Number-13: 978-0-415-65347-3 (Paperback)
International Standard Book Number-13: 978-0-415-97947-4 (Hardcover)
Library of Congress Card Number 2006006585

Library of Congress Cataloging-in-Publication Data

Akonor, Kwame.
Africa and IMF conditionality : the unevenness of compliance, 1983-2000 / by Kwame Akonor.
p. cm. -- (African studies : history, politics, economics, and culture)
Includes bibliographical references and index.
ISBN 0-415-97947-1 (alk. paper)
1. Structural adjustment (Economic policy)--Ghana. 2. Ghana--Politics and government--1979-2001. 3. International Monetary Fund--Ghana. I. Title. II. Series: African studies (Routledge (Firm)) III. Series.

HC1060.A57 2006
338.9667009'049--dc22 2006006585

Visit the Taylor & Francis Web site at
http://www.taylorandfrancis.com

and the Routledge Web site at
http://www.routledge-ny.com

Contents

List of Tables

List of Abbreviations

AFRC	Armed Forces Revolutionary Council
ARPB	Association of Recognized Professional Bodies
BOP	Balance of Payments
CDR	Committees for the Defense of the Revolution
CMB	Cocoa Marketing Board
COCOBOD	Cocoa Board
CPP	Convention Peoples' Party
CVC	Citizens' Vetting Committee
ERP	Economic Recovery Program
ESAF	Enhanced Structural Adjustment Facility
GBA	Ghana Bar Association
GDP	Gross Domestic Product
GPRTU	Ghana Private Road Transport Union
IFIs	International Financial Institutions
II	International Institutions
ILO	International Labor Organization
IMF	International Monetary Fund
JFM	June Fourth Movement
NCP	National Convention Party

NDC	National Democratic Congress
NDM	New Democratic Movement
NEC	National Electoral Commission
NERC	National Economic Review Committee
NLC	National Liberation Council
NPP	New Patriotic Party
NRC	National Redemption Council
NUGS	National Union of Ghana Students
PAMSCAD	Program of Actions to Mitigate the Social Costs of Adjustment
PDC	Peoples' Defence Committee
PNDC	Provisional National Defence Council
PNP	Peoples' National Party
PP	Progress Party
PRGF	Poverty Reduction and Growth Facility
PRSP	Poverty Reduction Strategy Paper
SAP	Structural Adjustment Program
SMC	Supreme Military Council
SOE	State-owned Enterprise
SSA	Sub Saharan Africa
TUC	Trades Union Congress
UNIGOV	Union Government
VAT	Value Added Tax
WDC	Workers' Defence Committee

Chronology of Key Events in Ghana's Political Economy

March 6, 1957	Ghana's independence from the British; Nkrumah is Premier
July 1, 1960	Inauguration of the First Republic
February 24, 1966	Coup d'etat by NLC overthrows Nkrumah
August 22, 1969	NLC hands over to civilians. Second Republic inaugurated. Busia's Progress Party (PP) rules
January 13, 1972	Coup d'etat by Col. Ignatius Kutu Acheampong and the NRC
October 1975	NRC superseded by Supreme Military Council (SMC)
July 5, 1978	Palace coup; Akuffo overthrows Acheampong and SMC II is ushered in.
June 4, 1979	Uprising by junior officers and AFRC led by Flt. Lt. J. J. Rawlings comes into power
September 24, 1979	Inauguration of Third Republic. Hilla Limann is President
December 31, 1981	Coup d'etat by Flight Lt. Rawlings' PNDC

January 1983	1.2 million Ghanaians expelled from Nigeria
April 1983	The ERP is announced; supported by World Bank and IMF
May 18, 1992	Lifting of ban on political parties
November 3, 1992	Presidential elections. Jerry Rawlings wins
December 29, 1992	Parliamentary elections. Opposition boycotts
January 7, 1993	Fourth Republic inaugurated
December 1996	Rawlings of NDC is re-elected. Opposition accepts results.
December 7, 2000	Rawlings NDC defeated. NPP's Kufuor is elected President
January 7, 2001	President Kufuor takes the oath of office becoming the first elected president in Ghana's history to succeed another elected president.

Acknowledgments

My friend and mentor Professor Ofuatey Kodjoe is largely instrumental for my successful completion of this manuscript. Professor Lenny Markovitz, inspired and pushed me to rethink and rewrite. Without the valuable contribution of these two, it would not have been possible to write this book. Dr. Eboe Hutchful also deserves special mention for his support and encouragement, and for providing me with invaluable information.

I am deeply indebted to the 'inside' sources who gave me access to confidential materials and resources, and to all persons whom I consulted both formally and informally on this project.

I dedicate this book to the Akonor family, and to Monique, Efua Asantewaa and Kwesi-Ansah Yeboa, with much love.

Chapter One
Introduction and Justification for Research

"Promises and pie-crust are made to be broken."
–Jonathan Swift, Polite Conversation

INTRODUCTION: RESEARCH OBJECTIVE

To reverse economic stagnation and decline of the 1980s, a majority of countries in sub Saharan Africa (SSA) turned to the International Monetary Fund (IMF, or Fund) and other International Financial Institutions (IFIs) for loans.[1] The IMF, which lends to member countries for balance-of-payment support, generally requires borrowing governments to make explicit commitments to implement remedial policies that the IMF deems essential to the amelioration of the borrowing country's external payments problems. The linking of the disbursement of a loan to "actions, or promises of actions, made by recipient governments only at the insistence of aid providers; measures that would not otherwise be undertaken, or not within the time frame desired by the providers" is referred to as conditionality[2] (Killick, 1998: 6; Mosley, 1992: 129).

IFI conditionality[3] typically consists of *(a)* policies to improve efficiency and resource allocation to correct the supply imbalance. These include removing barriers to competition and real market prices, removing state subsidies and ending government monopolies (i.e., privatization), and reforming overvalued currency; *(b)* policies to accelerate economic growth[4] to correct the demand imbalance. Examples are stimulating export production by lowering tariffs, eliminating quotas, and removing exchange controls (Killick et al., 1984). Together, these policy reform conditions have become known as Structural Adjustment Programs (SAPs).[5]

Conditionality, then, is a compensation mechanism that allows IFIs, such as the IMF,[6] to monitor behavior and provide incentives for compliance with the policies that are part of its programs.[7]

While this manuscript addresses questions of compliance with IMF conditionality generally, its main scholarly contribution is that it systematically analyzes noncompliance[8] by explicitly taking into account the borrowing government's domestic political environment. This study asks: When and why do recipient governments deviate, even if only temporarily, from the terms of IMF conditionality? Why do some adjusting countries,[9] while complying with loan conditions, adopt policies that have the effect of neutralizing or undermining SAPs? In short, what causes an adjusting government to risk a rupture in its SAP, and thus its relationship with the IMF?

Studying when and why states become noncompliant with SAPs is important because it broadens our understanding of the relationship between compliance with International Institutions (IIs) and domestic politics. To be sure, a plethora of studies on IMF conditionality exists,[10] yet none has attempted a systematic analysis on why states relax or discontinue policies that they have agreed to implement. The willful transfer of domestic economic policymaking by states, particularly developing countries, to IFIs, has caused some commentators to assert that most states now only have de jure, and not de facto, economic sovereignty; in that they are incapable of carrying out their traditional role as a buffer—that of protecting their domestic economies from deleterious policies of international institutional decisions and rules (Cox; 1996, Ould Mey, 1998). This manuscript is significant in that it allows us to begin specifying more precisely the factors and conditions that cause weak and peripheral states to exert influence and policy autonomy. In other words, since conditionality greatly weakens the economic autonomy of recipient countries, our study on when and why noncompliance with conditionalities take place will shed light on the mix of domestic variables that cause member states to shift the locus for economic decision and action back from IFIs.

This study also has topical and empirical import. In many ways, current controversies that have embroiled the IMF center on the Fund's use of conditionality in lending. But how can conditionality be reformed if we have no way of explaining how the policy changes are implemented, or when they fail to be implemented? Although he deals with a different set of questions, Graham Bird makes this point best. He says,

> "If the ultimate objective of policy conditionality is to improve the economic performance of countries to which it is applied, then it is insufficient to design a program which is appropriate in merely economic

terms. Thought also needs to be given to the circumstances in which it is most likely to be implemented."(1998: 91).

Perhaps in response to its numerous critics, the IMF (in March 2001) began a process of reviewing the conditions attached to its financing, with the aim to ensure that conditionality in Fund-supported programs reflects and reinforces national "ownership" (of reforms), and leads to sustained implementation of country economic reforms. A year later (September 2002) new conditionality guidelines were agreed upon.

This manuscript therefore carries a broader hope that explaining why states become noncompliant can make the process of international monetary cooperation more desirable and ensure that loan conditionality becomes more pragmatic.

THEORETICAL FRAMEWORK AND SUBSTANTIVE FOCUS

Several works in the social sciences have tackled in one way or the other the question of state compliance, or the lack thereof, with international institutional decisions and rules, but the answers provided thus far, especially in explaining why noncompliance occurs, have been inadequate and/or superficial.

A survey of the basic perspectives in International Relations (IR) quickly reveals the theoretical shortcomings. Realists, for instance, ascribe compliance and noncompliance to the effect of state power and interests. They argue that IIs are merely management tools of powerful states with "minimal influence on state behavior" (Mearsheimer 1994/95: 7). IIs are created and shaped by states and hence are a reflection of the interests of states (Mearsheimer 1990, Waltz 1979). States therefore become noncompliant if their core interests are threatened and/or if they cannot maximize their relative power over other states (Mearsheimer 1994/95: 25). There are two main problems with the realist paradigm as it relates to this study. First, while the theory may explain compliance and noncompliance behavior of powerful states toward IIs, it cannot adequately explain the same for small and poorer countries. The fact is a majority of smaller and poorer members of the IMF lack the voting power and capacity necessary to exercise any formal influence or ability to hold the institution to account.[11] Moreover, if there were a case in IR where II rules can influence state behavior, then it is IMF conditionality. To be sure, there are variations in the way states comply with IMF conditionality; nonetheless, IMF conditionality can and does influence state beliefs and strategies (Boorman 2001: 24).

Second, while realist perspectives may explain why SAPs are structured the way they are—i.e., the strong and dominant actors determine the structure of the international economic system—realist theory does not shed light on why weak states often fail to comply with SAPs. Realist theory would suggest that weak states would have no option but to comply with the SAP.

Liberal institutionalists (such as Keohane 1984, Oye 1986) on the other hand argue that compliance is produced by the fact that IIs, overtime, generate a web of interactions which "once established, will be difficult either to eradicate or drastically to rearrange" (Keohane and Nye 1989: 55). A state thus suffers reputational damage if it becomes noncompliant. However, this argument is also unsatisfactory because it cannot account for persistent noncompliance by states or for the variation in the degree to which IIs influence states. As Lisa Martin (1998) concedes,

> "understanding variation in institutional effects is the key challenge for institutionalist theory today. To explain this variation, we require a finer-grained understanding of the mechanisms through which institutions might exert their effects, and of the conditions under which these mechanisms are effective" (p. 755).

In order to resolve this difficulty, social constructivists[12] have attempted to locate compliance in the identity and interests of states as they are mutually constructed. Compliance, they argue, are not based on consequentialist calculus but on considerations of appropriateness (March and Olsen 1998: 949–950). A state complies with IIs because it internalizes "shared expectations about appropriate behavior" (Finnemore and Sikkink 1998: 951). But constructivism too is problematic. If consensual norms shape behavior why do states that belong to the same international regime exhibit different behaviors at different times? (Bandura 1986: 410). Moreover, how do we account for states with multiple identities, and from where do state identities originate? (Wildavsky 1987). At the end of the day we find that constructivism does not tell us very much on when and why states comply with international rules, and definitely not why they become noncompliant.

International legal scholars such as Burley (1993), Chayes and Chayes (1993 and 1995), Henkin (1979), Hurd (1999), and Weiss and Jacobson (1998) have all examined in some fashion what motivates states to follow international norms, rules, and commitments. What unites these authors is the thesis that enforcement plays little or no role in achieving and maintaining international compliance (Downs, Rocke, and Barsoom 1996). Known as the managerialist perspective, this approach insists that preferences are not predetermined but evolve over time and that norms are regulative rules that states would abide by. They maintain that breakdown in compliance usually occurs as a result of defective contracts or a lack of effective administrative and technical capacities (Weiss and Jacobson 1998). In other words, noncompliance with international agreement (if and when it occurs) is to be viewed not as willful and premeditated actions of the state but rather as anomalies brought on by incomplete contracts and/or domestic incapacities. IFIs and their sympathizers have used this domestic incapacity argument to justify mediocre reform results in SSA. Studies by the World Bank (1995) and Sahn, Dorosh, and Younger (1988), for example, have concluded that weak economic performance is not the result of bad policy but rather due to a lack of necessary institutional and human capacity.

Chayes and Chayes (1993), writing on compliance, argue that states enter into international agreements[13] with a propensity to comply. First, state policy analysis and decision making, they argue, are not cost free. So rather than continuously reassessing decisions to maximize utility, for efficiency reasons states often settle for a "satisficing" output. Second, they argue that states enter into agreements because they believe them to be in their interests. They point to the elaborate process of consultations and negotiations both domestically and inter-governmentally as guarantees that state interests are met at the time of treaty ratification and signing. Third, they believe that states are predisposed to carry out their international agreements rather than be obsessed with calculation of national interests because treaties are the acceptable norms of international behavior. Chayes and Chayes point out that one of the fundamental norms of international law is *pacta sunt servanda* (treaties are to be obeyed) and they find it:

> "not conceivable that foreign ministries and government leaders could devote time and energy on the scale they do to preparing, drafting, negotiating, and monitoring treaty obligations unless there is an assumption that entering into a treaty commitment ought to and does constrain the state's own freedom of action and an expectation that the other parties to the agreement will feel similarly constrained" (Chayes and Chayes 1993: 76).

So if states are inclined to honor their agreements why does noncompliance occur? For Chayes and Chayes (1993) noncompliance, when it occurs (and it rarely does), is not a willful output based on cost/benefit analysis by states but a good-faith lapse to which a state has no control. The first issue that may lead to noncompliance problems is the presence of language ambiguity in a treaty text. Another issue arises when the domestic capacity to affirm an obligation is lacking (as is often the case in treaties requiring scientific and technical endowment). Also, significant changes in the socioeconomic environment (e.g. refugee influx) may complicate compliance.

There are a number of problems with the managerialist thesis, especially as presented by Chayes and Chayes (1993, 1995). The assumptions that international agreements are self-enforcing, or that states need not enter into a treaty that does not conform to its interests, are *prima facie* axiomatic, but need qualification if we are to understand compliance/non compliance with IMF agreements. First, although the IMF does not directly enforce obligations, as stated earlier, finances are disbursed in phases or canceled to ensure compliance. Second, managerialists are incorrect to assume away voluntary defection. Managerialists will have us believe that countries would not deliberately violate conditionality terms. And compliance violations, if they occur, will be results of ambiguities in IMF conditionality or capacity problems at home, but not cost and benefit calculations by the state. But it is hard to agree with this analysis because IMF conditionality is pretty specific and policy actors do not have much latitude in interpreting its meanings. Policy prescriptions like "devaluation" or "wage freeze," for example, do not have multiple meanings. This point is further reinforced by the fact that the "extensive interagency vetting" that managerialists insist will help align national positions with domestic interests is virtually nonexistent in most SSA adjusting countries. To the contrary, most adjusting countries accept IMF conditionality with little or no domestic debate of its merits (Akonor 2001).

International Economics also provides insights into state compliance and noncompliance with II agreements. The discipline's principal-agent (PA) model is particularly germane to this manuscript.[14] PA refers to the problem of resource allocation that arises because contracts that will induce Agents (A) to act in the Principal's (P) interest are impossible to write or expensive to oversee (Sappington 1991, Grossman and Hark 1983, Douglas 1989). In general, PA relationships have the following characteristics:

1. One party (*A*) is contracted to do the bidding of another (*P*).
2. One party (usually *A*) knows more than the other about some important variable.
3. Some form of incentive and monitoring mechanism is put in place by *P* to ensure that *A* does what it was hired to do and/or that the situation of asymmetric information does not lead to moral hazard or other opportunistic behavior by *A* (Killick 1997: 485–487).

As it applies to this manuscript, the PA problem "is how principals (in this case, donors) can design contracts which embody rewards that make it in the interests of agents (recipient governments) to further the principals' objectives" (Killick 1997: 487). For the purposes of this manuscript I will make the following assumptions based on the PA framework. First, assume that adjusting countries have voluntarily and deliberately transferred economic policy authority to the IMF (condition I above). Second, assume that neither the IMF nor the adjusting countries have complete knowledge of all the important variables necessary to ensure compliance with conditionality. In fact, the adjusting countries will always know more about what it has done or intends to do than the IMF (condition II above) (Killick 1998: 102). The third assumption (stemming from condition III above) is that adjusting countries will comply with IMF conditionality if the incentive value (in this case international capital plus sound policy prescriptions) offered is greater than the participation costs (be it political or otherwise). This manuscript accepts the implied premise of this assumption: that decision outcomes to comply with conditionality are based on a cost/benefit calculation by recipient countries. This manuscript goes further by insisting that the incentive value is a necessary but not sufficient condition to induce compliance. We argue that no matter how beneficial or attractive an incentive is it would not suffice to induce an adjusting country to comply if that government believes that continuation of policy will jeopardize its political tenure.

The few writers who have tried to answer the question of state noncompliance with IMF conditionality using the PA conceptual framework have left some terrain uncharted. For example, Killick (1998, 1997), in his study on twenty-one developing countries, found support for the overall hypothesis that (1) donors are unwilling or unable to punish non-implementation, and that (2) domestic politics usually prevails over donor pressures when "serious donor-recipient disagreements" exist. He goes on to argue for a new model of donor-recipient relationships based on principles of ownership, selectivity, support, and dialogue.

Killick's (1998: 151–156, and 1997: 492) allusion to high political costs as a factor to noncompliance is suggestive but has minimal explanatory value. First, the general notion that divergent objectives between adjusting countries and the donor countries create implementation problems may not also hold. It is perfectly plausible that a country may have an opposite agenda to that of the donor and yet agree to conditionality. This can occur, for example, in cases where the lure of financial offer is substantial and the borrowing country's regime is divided and confused on its policy alternatives. Moreover, as Killick correctly notes, some level of divergence in donor and government policy objectives is normal (1997: 488).

Yet he fails to define and operationalize when such disagreements or differences are "serious" enough to lead to noncompliance. The second problem with Killick's proposition is that it is vague on which domestic political variables impact compliance. Killick maintains that governments act based on perceptions of their interests which "in turn reflect the historical and institutional context in which they are located, the specifics of the political systems, and the quality of their leaderships" (1998: 152). This explanation is superficial; it fails to provide clues as to how and why the domestic factors he identifies cause noncompliance. What is relevant for explanatory analysis is not the political settings, political systems, and regime type, but rather how specific factors or conditions within the political settings, political systems, and regime type intermix to cause noncompliance.

Mosley, Harrigan, and Toye (1998) also discuss the influence of national politics on compliance with donor conditionality using four (not mutually exclusive) explanations. First, commitment to reform is viewed as a function of regime type. Democratic states, it is argued, are ill suited to implement and sustain economic reform because they have a need to placate interest groups (Mosley et al. 1998: 145, Lal 1985: 33). A second domestic factor that may impinge upon conditionality is the life span of the regime. A new regime is seen as possessing fresh energy and leverage that may be brought to bear both at the loan negotiation and policy implementation stages. The implication is that once a regime's "honeymoon" period ends it has a harder time carrying through with reforms, especially when the positive impact of reforms is not being realized. (Ka and van de Walle 1994: 290–359). An alternative explanation is found in a country's historical record of policy reform. This thesis holds that prior success with reform generates consensus to further future reform. Likewise, experience with misguided policies will lead countries to opt for conditionality. The fourth reason given for the centrality of domestic influence on conditionality has to do with the proliferation and power of interest groups. Sophisticated and dominant anti-reform groups are able to frustrate or disrupt implementation of conditionality through civil disobedience and other pressure-building tactics. The idea here is that interest group pressures can and do impede a government's ability to implement conditionality.

Mosley et al. is more successful at outlining central domestic variables that may influence compliance; however, like Killick they fail to explain when, how, and why noncompliance comes about. In other words, even if one concedes that a country's economic history and oppositional politics, as well as the regime's structure, are important factors that may impact decisions about conditionality, we still would not have a hypothesis on how the variables intermix to cause noncompliance.

STATEMENT OF ARGUMENT

Based on the above discussion, I make the following assumptions within which this study will be situated.

First, a distinction needs to be made between noncompliance that arises as a result of an impossible target, adverse shocks, or unfeasible policy (Mosley et al. 1998: 140) and one that arises because a government chose not to comply either by stalling or aborting reform. I am concerned only with the latter. The political economy of noncompliance assumes that economic policy derives from political choices.

Second, I assume that government's principal goal is to retain power (Bird 1998: 99), therefore governments will make choices based on cost/benefit calculations, with an underlying objective to retain political power.[15] To borrow the language of March and Olsen, my study posits that a logic of political power consequences will perpetually trump a logic of compliance appropriateness when it comes to IFI conditionality.

Third, we also need to distinguish between commitment to reform and failure to implement required reform. This manuscript seeks to analyze the latter. It does not question the underlying commitment of a borrowing country to implement reform. Moreover, as some studies have indicated, governments do not equivocate when it comes to commitment to reform. That is to say, regardless of their domestic situation government's go to donors with a firm position to either commit or not (Mosley, Harrigan, and Toye, 1991: 141). I will therefore assume that governments are committed to reform, when they approach the IFIs.

If these assumptions hold true how does one answer our research question on why governments stall or abort conditionality? I hypothesize that the greater the gap between the political cost of compliance and the economic benefit of compliance, the greater the likelihood of noncompliance. In other words, an adjusting country will become noncompliant once it perceives its domestic political cost to outweigh the economic benefits. The immediate challenge then is to specify the circumstances that may lead to high political costs. I posit that political costs are high when the political survival of a regime is at stake. Thus, placing my argument within the rational choice framework, I identify the survival drive and desire of a political regime to maintain political power as a major explanatory factor on why noncompliance with IMF conditionality occurs. I argue that two such critical moments when there is a need to muster domestic support in order to stay in power (and when we can expect noncompliance) is periods prior to elections and periods of elite[16] conflict/instability.[17]

PRE-ELECTION NONCOMPLIANCE

The first explanatory variable that I argue will cause noncompliance is pre-election spending. Conditionality as noted above is austere in nature and necessarily includes reductions in social expenditures. Yet social spending is not only subject to politics but is considered a successful survival strategy by politicians (Ames 1987, Stallings 1992). As the literature on Political Business Cycles (PBC), (Heckelman and Berument 1998, Nordhaus 1975, Rogoff and Sibert 1988, McCallum and Bennett 1978, Beck 1982) demonstrates, politicians manipulate macroeconomic policy 'opportunistically' to enhance their prospects of re-election, even though any economic changes will be short-lived. In other words, incumbent governments bent on keeping their jobs and/or party in power will attempt to manipulate macroeconomic policy during election cycles in ways that are considered beneficial to the electorate in general and their constituents in particular. As it relates to noncompliance, I argue that though conditional IMF credit typically constrains discretionary expenditure policies, thereby preventing opportunistic policy making, an incumbent government in advance of competitive elections will boost their popularity and reelection chances by increasing public expenditure or lowering taxes. Either strategy is certain to violate the terms of conditional lending to which the government had consented to with the IMF because conditionality generally requires contractionary monetary and fiscal policies to restrain domestic demand.

But PBC theories are not without critics. There are those who charge that voters are not as myopic as the model assumes. That assessment is correct if we consider only the first generation of PBC models Nordhaus (1975), Tufte (1978) and MacRae (1977), which generally assumed that voters are naive and retrospective.[18] Recently, however, theoretical developments in the literature have adjusted these earlier models. Voters are now assumed to be rational and forward-looking. Rogoff and Sibert (1988), for example, argue that voters need not be myopic for PBC to occur. They maintain that economics matter to rational voters[19] and voter's reward incumbents who are competent. Yet competence is not public information (asymmetric information). Uninformed voters can only infer incumbents' competence by observing economic data, which are generally available after a time lag. This, they argue, provides politicians with an incentive to manipulate voter attitudes by pursuing expansionary policies before elections, which in turn signals "competence"to the electorate. Similarly, Persson and Tabellini (1990), argue that voters are not backward-looking, and yet they are influenced repeatedly. Their study found that rational voters do not learn from past experiences and do not adjust their behavior over subsequent business cycles.

This leads us to the issue of whether politicians possess the capacity and cynicism to manipulate the economy in such a timely fashion, and whether incumbent governments, particularly in weaker economies, can play with the political business cycle in the same way as their industrial counterparts. The evidence for this is mixed in the industrial world. Paldam (1979, 1981) did not find support for the hypothesis in his empirical test on a number of OECD countries. Rather than spending in the election year, he found increases in the governmental expenditures in the second year after the election. In contrast, Grier (1989) found significant support for the thesis.

But the empirical evidence from developing countries tends to overwhelmingly support the predictions made in the PBC literature. Here are a few cross-country studies that make this point. Ames (1987) in a study of 17 Latin American countries over 35 years, found significant increases in total public sector expenditures in electoral years. Schuknecht (1996) also found evidence for political business cycles in a study of 35 countries between 1970 and 1992. Block (2002) presents further evidence of a political business cycle in both fiscal and monetary policy in a cross-section of Sub-Saharan African countries. Indeed, there are analysts who argue that PBCs are more likely to occur in developing countries than in developed countries. In justifying this proposition, Haggard and Kaufman said:

> "Many of the political and institutional characteristics of the advanced industrial states that mitigate the political business cycle are absent in the developing country context. . . . These include, among other things, more informed publics, more independent media coverage of economic policy, more institutionalized forms of consultation which lengthen the time horizons of affected social groups, and extensive welfare systems that cushion the costs of unemployment. Given generally lower levels of income and extensive poverty, electoral support in the developing world might plausibly be linked to the government's ability to deliver short-term material benefits" (Haggard and Kaufman, 1989, 241–2).

Moreover, it is possible to test PBC theories using a single country case study. Numerous single country case studies have been done in developing countries, most of which corroborate the PBC thesis. Schady's (2000) study of Peru from 1991–95, Krueger and Turan's (1993) study of Turkey in the period 1950–1980, Gonzalez's (1999) study in Mexico from period 1958–1997, and Ben-Porath (1975) study on Israel over the period 1952–73 are but a few examples.

Schuknecht (1996) argues that there is overwhelming empirical support for PBC in developing countries because the weak checks and balances in the developing countries means the incumbent has more control over monetary and fiscal policy. Now whether such "pre-election budget antics" (Rogoff 1990, 21) help or hurt politicians in developing countries is an interesting question that remains unresolved in the literature (and one which is beyond the scope of our research question).

But what about authoritarian[20] military regimes, or countries where electoral politics are not practiced? This question implies that only politicians in democracies are sensitive to utility calculations of their constituents. This assumption is not only incorrect, but it misses the point. To be sure, authoritarian governments do not have electoral pressures to worry about and can use repressive means to implement reform. Even so, they are accountable to, and need support from certain segment of, the public. Senior officers, for example, are indispensable to the political survival of authoritarian military regimes (Wintrobe 1998: 341). Moreover, the argument here is not so much on regime type as it is on the political survival of a regime. The question then ought to be this: When is the political survival of an authoritarian regime, or any political system, at stake? This leads us to our next variable: "elite instability."

ELITE-INSTABILITY-INDUCED NONCOMPLIANCE

If I maintain our earlier assumption that governments seek to maintain and maximize political power, it is safe to say that the survival risk for political regimes is highest when there is elite conflict.[21] I maintain that the support of the political elite is key to the survival of any political regime, democratic or otherwise. If this assumption is correct, then any form of inter-elite violence, be it a coup, alleged plots, or forced resignations will create high political cost for the political regime because the political life of the regime is threatened. The regime will now have an urgent need to muster more support (or equivalently reduce opposition) from the population, or at least its key constituents, to maximize its chance of survival.

According to Frey and Eichenberger (1994), a regime can shore up domestic support if it increases its utility to the population or core bloc. And there are three strategies that a regime can employ to increase its utility to the population. The regime may stimulate economic growth; provide special privileges to powerful groups (bribing as positive sanctions) or utilize little suppression (or negative sanctions). Of course, the action taken will depend on the regime type and/or political system and the resources available, but in Africa, time and again, we find that politicians have consolidated their power through the discretionary use (or should say I abuse) of expenditure policies to special groups, firms or individuals.[22] I argue that an adjusting country that embarks on unprioritized expenditure policies, such as free or subsidized goods, excess military spending or public investment spending to shore up domestic support, will become noncompliant with the terms of IMF conditionality because monetary expansion and the budget deficit[23] will increase.[24]

RESEARCH DESIGN AND DATA COLLECTION PLANS

The methodology employed in this research is a structured and focused 'within-case' comparison. This entails a sequenced and detailed examination and comparison of the compliance and noncompliance by the government of Ghana over a specified period (1983–1990). Specifically, this research deals with questions of Ghana's compliance[25] with IMF conditionality—to what extent did it comply, how did it manage compliance, what patterns of noncompliance exist, and what conditions lead it to renege?

Each step in this research effort attempted to specify the cause-effect linkages between the independent and dependent variables and made use of generalizations derived from theory.[26] In the case of Ghana, a sequenced examination of the policy behavior of the same actors and/or regime under different conditions over time, allowed for a more accurate identification of the conditions under which noncompliance occurred.

I chose the Ghanaian experience for the following reasons. First, the economic recovery program (ERP) it began in 1983 has been one of the most aggressive and extensive there is on the African scene (Jeong 1996, Leechor 1994). Mosley et al. observed that "the Ghana Government has taken full responsibility for the ERP/SAP, and has not resorted to criticizing the Fund or Bank when reforms run into difficulties" (1991: 184). This fact—that Ghana is a "good client"—made it an interesting place to find explanations for noncompliance.

Second, Ghana has been both a military dictatorship and a civilian democracy since 1983, thus making it possible to diachronically compare its noncompliance at different historical periods. This fact is particularly instructive as we consider the relationship between elite conflict, political survival strategies and noncompliance. Our study will cover the 1983 to 2000 period.

The dependent variable: The outcome that I wish to explain is noncompliance, defined as policy behavior that is contrary to IMF conditionality. The process of noncompliance with Fund agreements, I hold, is not an all-or-nothing proposition and can occur selectively and intermittently. Non-compliance then is the halting, reversing, or aborting of IMF-approved policy stipulations by an adjusting country that leads to a suspension in the IMF program or a reprimand by the IMF.

I adopt Tony Killick's (1998:6) definition of conditionality as "actions, or promises of actions, made by recipient governments only at the insistence of aid providers; measures that would not otherwise be undertaken, or not within the time frame desired by the providers." The Fund is an appropriate selection for this research because all its policy programs require ceilings on domestic credit creation and public spending (Bird 1998: 94). Thus, unlike its sister institution, the World Bank, where noncompliance with conditionality normally takes years to monitor, the Fund's conditions can be monitored after very few lags, thus making it easier for us to document noncompliance. (Mosley, Harrigan, and Toye 1998: 68).

Our independent variables are elections and elite instability.

An election is a procedure that allows members of an organization or community to choose representatives who will hold positions of authority within it. I will consider nation-wide general, parliamentary, or presidential elections.

For elite instability, I adopted Morrison and Stevenson's (1971: 349) definition as "the violent removal of persons from the command positions they hold in political institutions, when the violence is directed by alternative functional elites."

DATA COLLECTION

This manuscript utilized qualitative data collection procedures (Marshall and Rossman, 1989) primarily document analysis, elite interview, and content analysis, to elicit, empirically, an explanation for Ghana's compliance and noncompliance with IMF conditionality. Here is how the research task was performed.

DOCUMENTATION OF IMF CONDITIONALITY AND COMPLIANCE ACTIVITY

I described and explained the extent to which Ghana was compliant with IMF conditionality. Ascertained how domestic political considerations and realities hindered or helped compliance.

DOCUMENTATION OF NONCOMPLIANCE ACTIVITY

I described the specific SAPs that conditioned grants from the IMF to Ghana during 1983 through 2000. Next, I assessed Ghana's performance against

IMF conditionality and specify the periods when Ghana was noncompliant. As noted earlier, ceilings on central bank credit and public spending are central to all IMF conditionality. I collected this data by examining the Bank of Ghana's[27] Monthly Statistical Bulletin as well as its Quarterly Balance Sheet and recorded its credit to the government. For public spending, we examined government documents such as the Government Budget, Finance Ministry Memos, parliamentary debates, speeches and probes, as well as local newspapers. The idea here was to record and specify the occurrence of extra-budgetary spending, unauthorized payments, and unprioritized public investment programs. One difficulty that arose with the study of conditionality was the problem of confidentiality. For instance, there are two key documents that proved invaluable to this study: the Letter of Intent sent to the Fund by the borrowing country, and the (IMF-owned) Poverty Reduction and Growth Facility (PRGF) Arrangement.[28] Unfortunately, only the former document is divulged to the public. To supplement the IMF Letter of Intent, I visited the Fund's Archives and Records Division to pore over its other publications on Ghana for the period under study. For insider and unavailable public information, interviews (some confidential) were conducted with key persons involved in the negotiation and implementation of adjustment. To this end, much of the discussions on the IMF negotiations are not fully sourced because they are based on confidential interviews and confidential IMF materials.

DOCUMENTATION OF ELECTION-INDUCED ACTIVITY

Three different time lags (18 months, 12 months, and 6 months) may be used to capture the impact of elections on policy (Berger and Woitek 1997: 11). I restricted the election variable to six months (election month included) because, generally, that is when election campaigning is at its peak. Using the information obtained in Step 1, I outlined the semi annual monetary aggregates for central bank credit to government and government spending during an election year and compared them with non-election years.

DOCUMENTATION OF ELITE INSTABILITY

Here, I operationalized elite instability using the following variables: Plots, Attempted Coups, Coups d'etat, and forced resignations (Morisson and Stevenson 1971). Plots are "events in which an announcement is made by the political elite that a plot to overthrow the government has been discovered" (p. 351); Attempted Coup is a failed coup d'etat; Coup d'etat was recorded as "an event in which the existing political regime is suddenly and illegally displaced by the action of relatively small, elite groups without any overt mass participation in the event" (p. 351). Forced resignations are said to occur when a large number of key decision-makers are pressured to vacate their command position against their wish.

Combing through Ghanaian newspaper archives and the Keesing's Record of World Events, I collected and analyzed event data on extra-legal government activity relating to the elite. Using the information obtained in Step 1, I then compared government spending and central bank credit six months prior to the occurrence of elite instability with monetary aggregates after elite instability.

Chapter Two

Ghana's Evolving Political Economy and the Conundrum of IMF Compliance: 1957–1983

"Poverty is the common lot of Ghanaians."
—Douglas Rimmer, Staying Poor: Ghana's Political Economy 1950–1990
Pergamon, Oxford, 1992.

INTRODUCTION

A proper understanding of why noncompliance with IMF conditionality occured in Ghana during the SAP periods must be based on a careful examination of the perception and role of the IMF in Ghana from 1957 (when Ghana become independent) to 1983 (when the SAPs began). Such an examination is important for two reasons. First, identifying the realm of IMF experiences at different points in Ghana's history (and with different regimes) allows us to have, not merely, a nuanced understanding of how the IMF is "imagined," "represented," or "thought of," by the political elite,[1] but more importantly how this perception could become a formidable barrier to compliance. Second, such an examination will provide the historical and empirical basis for the analysis of how political, rather than economic, logics prevailed during Ghana's SAP periods.

The chapter is divided into two sections. The first section examines the historical evolution of Ghana's political economy and how that impacted successive government's attitudes toward compliance, or noncompliance, with IMF conditionality. Section two examines the factors that led Rawlings' PNDC to adopt IMF loans and conditionalities, despite its earlier populist strategy.

I argue that the post-independent Ghanaian political regimes, particularly Nkrumah's (1957–1966) made an ideological and nationalistic investment against IMF conditionality. I also show that the negative association with IMF conditionality was also intertwined with leadership fears of losing political power (usually through a coup). I argue further that Ghana's changing political economy, for the worse, (and changes in government) caused the negative association with IMF conditionality to gradually (if reluctantly) change.

THE NKRUMAH GOVERNMENT: 1957–1966

Nkrumah's socialist ideological makeup,[2] combined with his anti-capitalist economic policies, made him deeply suspicious and ambivalent toward foreign capital and its related institutions (including the IMF). Having waged a successful struggle for Ghana's political independence, Nkrumah was determined not to sacrifice the country's economic independence at the altars of any International Financial Institution (IFI). The nationalistic spirit with which Nkrumah confronted the IMF essentially set the parameters around which subsequent regimes (democratic or otherwise) dealt with that institution.

Ghana became a member of the IMF on September 20, 1957. Six months prior, on March 6, 1957, under the leadership of Dr. Kwame Nkrumah, Ghana (formerly Gold Coast) had become the first sub-Saharan African country to attain its independence from a colonial power, Britain.

At the time of its independence, Ghana had apparently good economic prospects: accumulated net foreign reserves of about $269 million; one of the highest income per head in SSA; the world's largest producer of cocoa; and substantial reserves of gold, bauxite, and magnesium. However, one can also argue that the characteristics of the economy (the dependence of its production system on imported inputs; its excessive dependence on primary exports for foreign exchange)[3] made such prospects tentative and especially vulnerable to trends in the international economy. Indeed as Rodney (1972) has noted, colonial economies (like Ghana's) were not designed, in terms of production and consumption, to benefit Africa and Africans, but rather Europeans. As mono-economies, the colonial economic structures were not oriented to diversification but rather focused on the production and export of a single commodity (be it agricultural or mineral), with prices determined by the external European market, thus making the whole colonial economic system highly dependent on external finances and demand (Rodney 1972).

Nkrumah's development vision was that of a socialist society with the state in control of all key aspects of the economy (Hutchful, 1987:

2–9). The Nkrumah Government's development strategy rested on the assumption that the state is the most critical agent to give a "big push" of industrial transformation. He wrote: "the vicious circle of poverty which keeps us in our rut of impoverishment, can only be broken by a massively planned industrial undertaking." (Nkrumah, 1963: 167). To give impetus to this vision, Nkrumah, in 1959, introduced a Five Year Development Plan in which forty-four % of all planned investment was to be carried out by the state. In an address to the first parliament of the Republic on 1st July 1960, he explained that the reliance on central planning was a means of turning Ghana into "a modern industrial nation providing opportunities for all and a standard of living comparable to any in the world." In 1964, he set up the State Enterprise secretariat (which he headed) to help regulate the activities of the "main economic pillars" of the state (i.e., the state enterprises).[4]

For Nkrumah, industrial growth was to be achieved through massive state intervention in the economy (with emphasis on import substitution). To that end, his development strategy was also decidedly anti-capitalist: it saw no role for local private capital (and hence the development of an indigenous capitalist class) and it was ambivalent toward foreign private capital. (Hutchful, 1987: 4–5). At one point, Nkrumah reminded Parliament that Ghana would be hampering its advance to socialism, if it encouraged the growth of Ghanaian private capitalism (Nkrumah quoted in Garlick 1971; 126).[5] Further, the Nkrumah government perceived foreign private capital as an encroachment on Ghana's economic independence, but one that was incapable of competing with interventionist state structures. Krobo Edusei, Nkrumah's Minister of Industries, voiced these prevailing nationalist sentiments when in 1962 he argued that:

> "Since December last year, Ghana has for the first time decided to exercise one of the weapons of economic sovereignty—import control! So long as this weapon is carefully and wisely yielded, our young and infant industries which are facing ruthless competition from long established and giant monopoly industries overseas, will be protected from dumping." (Edusei, 1962: 198–199)

Nkrumah financed his development programs with loans, supplier's credit,[6] and reserves inherited from the colonial regime, and mainly with revenues from cocoa exports. But the world price of cocoa did not hold up for long, as world prices began to collapse precipitously soon after Ghana's independence. In 1958 for instance, the London price of cocoa was $977 per ton, by 1965 it had more than halved to a mere $400 per ton. Despite the adverse earnings in cocoa revenue the Ghanaian government continued to spend, leading to massive budget and balance of payments deficits and a looming economic crisis (Krassowski, 1974: 90). Between 1959 and 1961 for example, the government surpassed its capital budget by 10%.[7] As Table I shows, this overspending affected the country's net foreign reserves, which had turned negative by 1965, and was causing Ghana acute balance of payments problems.

In 1964, the Fund, concerned about the rapidly deteriorating economic developments in Ghana sent its Executive Board to visit Ghana and advise the Nkrumah government. The Executive Board issued a statement that read:

> "In order to prevent further deterioration in the domestic and external situation the Fund considers that there is an urgent need to contain domestic, particularly government expenditure. Total government expenditure should be limited to an amount that can be financed from non-inflationary sources." (Ghana, 1964: 61).

Nkrumah's government did not pay heed to the IMF until a year later, in May 1965 (as Ghana's economic situation worsened), the Nkrumah government, in an about-face (given his fierce anti-imperialist and anti-capitalist rhetoric and actions), set out to consult the Fund[8] for financial assistance, and to formally invite the Fund's mission to Ghana. As Nkrumah's Finance Minister explained, the Fund was needed to assist Ghana in preparing a program, which would enable the country to renegotiate its credit. (Hutchful, 1987: 45). Addressing Parliament on September 10, 1965, Amoako Atta (Nkrumah's Finance Minster) said:

> "We have now reached a stage where our reserves cannot be run down any further without endangering the stability of the Cedi. It was for this and other reasons, particularly the catastrophic drop in the price of cocoa, that the Government decided recently to invite a mission from the International Monetary Fund, of which Ghana is a member, to come to this country and to assist us to prepare a programme which would enable us to re-negotiate some of the suppliers' credits which we have contracted. The object of this exercise is to re-negotiate with the foreign suppliers, through their governments, to extend the period of repayment of these credits and to reduce the burden of debt servicing. This would make it possible to use proportionately more of the revenues we are able to raise and the foreign exchange we earn in the further development of our country." (Ghana, 1965: 2)

According to the IMF, the Ghanaian economy was severely overstrained and needed to undertake immediate economic adjustment. The IMF asked the Nkrumah government to comply with the following measures as part of a package in exchange for financial credit:

1. Government expenditure, recurrent and capital, should be limited to an amount that can be covered by Government revenue and by non-inflationary borrowing.
2. A temporary halt should be placed on the launching of new projects financed by suppliers' credits of a short- or medium-term nature.
3. Steps should be taken to cut domestic demand, including a cut in the producer price of cocoa.
4. The dependence of State enterprises on subsidies from the Central Government should be stopped.
5. The control of the public purse and the commitment of public funds should be centralized and strengthened.
6. The liberal attitude toward foreign investment found in the Capital Investments Act should be made more manifest in public policies.
7. Import licensing should be based on a strict system of priorities. Some global quotas should be introduced, and licenses issued should be honored promptly by all relevant agencies of the Government.
8. The bilateral and barter arrangements should be reconsidered with a view to reducing their harmful impact on the Ghana economy (Ghana, 1965: 3–4; Hutchful, 1987: 42–45)

Nkrumah's government reacted to the IMF conditionalities in three ways. First, it kept its negotiations with the Fund a secret, for five months. It was not until the *Economist* ran a story in late August 1965 that Nkrumah's government briefed Parliament (Hutchful, 1987: 45).

Second, Nkrumah's government began to implement some of the Fund's 'prior actions,'[9] (such as reducing the expenditure in its Seven-year budget plan and cutting the producer price of cocoa). But instead of fully crediting the economic logic of IMF conditionality for the adopted prior actions (hence making compliance a deliberate choice), the Nkrumah government attributed the policy actions to the "financial prudence emphasized by 'Osagyefo'[10] rather than the dictates of the Fund" (Hutchful, 1987: 52) (hence making compliance 'serendipitous').[11]

Third, Nkrumah's government wanted to wish away the ideological disagreement with the Fund and the nationalistic investment that had made foreign capital (and by extension IMF conditionality) so unattractive a development option. What Nkrumah took for granted was that his inward-looking state-led import-substitution strategy, which involved a multiplicity of trade and exchange controls and restrictions, went against the fundamental economic ideology that the IMF had been established to uphold. It must be noted that one of the central operating goals of the IMF is to develop and maintain multilateralism in international payments; thus trade restrictions and exchange controls, as Nkrumah's CPP was practicing, defies the logic for which it (the IMF) was created.[12] On February 22, 1966 (two days before Nkrumah's government was overthrown in a coup), the Finance Minister in a speech to Parliament urged The Fund, and other creditors, to set aside "ideological differences" and help Ghana find economic solutions that are mutually beneficial to both parties. He said:

> "As the Fund and Bank are aware, we can differ on the details of the recommendations without disagreeing on its major aspects . . . We are prepared to put our house in order and have indeed initiated the necessary measures to this end. We do hope therefore that the Fund and Bank will now show us their good faith by forgetting ideological differences and sitting at the negotiating table with us to see a solution to [our economic] problem to our mutual benefit." (Ghana, 1966: 3)

What is striking about Nkrumah's late dealings with the IMF is that his government agreed in "principle" to the economic policy recommendations of the Fund (Hutchful, 1987: 46), yet for political and ideological reasons Nkrumah was reluctant to associate fully with those polices.

As the negotiations dragged on, and before any IMF supported reform could take place, Nkrumah's government was overthrown by the National Liberation Council (NLC) headed by Lt. Gen. Joseph Ankrah. Hutchful (1987:3) suggests that

> "one of the immediate factors precipitating the coup was the disagreement between the International Monetary Fund and The Nkrumah Government on how to resolve the [economic] crisis in Ghana's "socialist' development."

So, quite early, since Ghana's independence, we begin to see the domestic political significance of IMF economic activity.

Table 1.1. Selected Macroeconomic Indicators in Ghana, 1960–1983

	Net Reserves as % of GDP	Nominal Exchange Rate (cedi/ US$)	Equilibrium Exchange Rate (cedi/ US$)	Measure Of Over-valuation	M2 Growth Rate (%)	Inflation Rate (%)	Fiscal Deficit % of GDP	Balance of Trade % of GDP
1960	21.2	0.71	0.71	0.00	13.3	0.9	-5.9	-7.1
1961	12.2	0.71	0.71	-0.09	6.3	6.2	-6.2	-9.2
1962	12.9	0.71	0.74	4.07	17.6	5.9	-8.7	-4.1
1963	12.1	0.71	0.77	7.41	10.0	5.6	-8.2	-6.4
1964	5.5	0.71	0.87	22.11	31.8	15.0	-8.2	-3.9
1965	-0.5	0.71	1.04	45.39	3.4	22.7	-5.9	-10.3
1966	-1.8	0.71	1.14	60.30	6.7	14.0	-2.8	-5.5
1967	-3.5	0.84	1.01	19.84	0.0	-9.7	-5.6	-4.7
1968	-2.6	1.02	1.07	4.84	9.4	10.7	-6.0	-2.4
1969	-5.2	1.02	1.09	6.65	11.4	6.5	-3.2	-1.9
1970	-1.1	1.02	1.05	2.52	10.3	3.0	-1.4	-0.7
1971	-0.4	1.03	1.10	6.90	9.3	8.8	-3.0	-5.0
1972	4.5	1.33	1.18	-17.62	42.6	10.6	-4.4	6.7
1973	6.1	1.17	1.26	-8.95	17.9	17.1	-4.8	7.0
1974	0.0	1.15	1.30	-5.82	27.8	18.8	-3.7	-0.7
1975	2.4	1.15	1.49	6.43	37.6	29.8	-6.4	3.3

(continued)

Table 1.1. Selected Macroeconomic Indicators in Ghana, 1960–1983 (continued)

	Net Reserves as % of GDP	Nominal Exchange Rate (cedi/ US$)	Equilibrium Exchange Rate (cedi/ US$)	Measure Of Over-valuation	M2 Growth Rate (%)	Inflation Rate (%)	Fiscal Deficit % of GDP	Balance of Trade % of GDP
1976	0.3	1.15	2.10	58.62	36.7	55.4	-9.5	1.6
1977	0.0	1.15	3.72	177.28	60	116.5	-6.6	0.3
1978	0.1	1.76	6.08	220.37	68.8	73.1	-8.5	0.9
1979	1.2	2.75	8.30	133.37	15.8	54.5	-6.5	1.0
1980	0.5	2.75	10.8	201.65	33.8	50.2	-4.0	0.3
1981	-0.3	2.75	21.52	563.57	51.3	116.5	-6.1	-1.5
1982	0.0	2.75	24.10	603.88	23.4	22.3	-5.4	-0.1
1983	-3.1	8.83	50.84	1278.70	40.2	122.8	-2.6	-0.3

Source: Frimpong-Ansah J.H. (1991) *The Vampire State in Africa*, pp. 160–169

THE NATIONAL LIBERATION COUNCIL (NLC) & THE BUSIA GOVERNMENT: 1966–1972

The intransigence of the Nkrumah regime towards the IMF contrasted sharply with the close collaboration of the NLC and, later, the Busia regimes.

THE NATIONAL LIBERATION COUNCIL (NLC)

The leaders of the 1966 coup,[13] composed of four army officers and four police officers, [14] established their new government around the National Liberation Council (NLC) and pledged an early return to a duly constituted civilian government, which they honored in October 1969.

The NLC set up a seven-member economic committee headed by Mr. E. N. Omaboe to correct the 'misguided economic and financial policies of the former Government.' The appointment of Omaboe, a leading figure in economic policy-making under Nkrumah, as chairman of the NLC's National Economic Committee is significant in that it exposes the internal economic rift within Nkrumah's government between technocrats, like Omaboe, who wanted to re-impose economic rationality into policymaking and ideologues, like Amoako Atta (the finance minister), who wanted political considerations to guide economic policy.

Four days after the coup, on February 28, 1966, an urgent cable from Albert Adomakoh, the Governor of the Bank of Ghana, was sent to P. P. Schweitzer, Managing Director of IMF, through Amon Nikoi, the IMF Executive Director for Ghana. The cable read:

> "We take this opportunity to inform you that the new government of Ghana, the National Liberation Council, wishes to take up negotiations with the Fund immediately for drawing on the Fund's resources to the amount equivalent to our gold tranche and first credit tranche. Under the same urgency and especially since part of the causes of our present financial difficulties is attributable to the serious fall in the world price of cocoa particularly during the last two years we would also like to draw the twenty-five per centum of quota allowed under the Compensatory Finance Scheme. We desire also to arrange for a standby credit equivalent to the second credit tranche for a period of one year beginning from the date of drawing. We are sure that the Fund appreciates the urgency of our need and will give this matter due attention. If at all possible we would like to have concluded these transactions not later than end of March. (Ghana Documents)

At the request of the NLC, a delegation of the Economic Committee, headed by Omaboe, left Ghana on May 13, 1966 to attend a meeting of the Executive Board of the IMF to apply for a loan and to explore the possibility of further economic aid to Ghana. On May 16, 1966, the NLC was able to secure $36.4 million from the IMF. In return, the NLC agreed to reduce government expenditure, restrict central bank financing, and to review the 1966/67 budget with the IMF (through its representative to be stationed in Accra, as well as two IMF budget experts, also to be stationed in Accra). (Hutchful, 1987: 67).

Between 1966 and 1969, the NLC complied with numerous IMF-directed stabilization programs (this marked, in earnest, the beginnings of IMF conditionality in Ghana). Below are a few examples:

1. Devaluation of the national currency (by thirty % against the U.S. dollar). Shortly before the devaluation of the cedi on July 8, 1967 the International Monetary Fund had announced on May 24, 1967, that it had approved a stand-by arrangement authorizing Ghana to draw up to $25,000,000 over the next year. On May 27, 1968, the I.M.F. announced another stand-by arrangement for $12,000,000 for the next 12 months.
2. Ceiling of central bank credit to Government at 159 million (cedis) ceiling of loans to private sector and commercial banks at 15.3 million (cedis)
3. The setting aside of 5 million new cedis[15] of the additional budgetary receipts arising from cocoa earnings for employment creation.
4. Wage increases not exceed a 5% ceiling.
5. Retrenchment of an estimated 60,000 workers in state-owned enterprises over the period
6. Phased liberalization of import and exchange control and removal of price controls and subsidies (Hutchful, 1987, Frimpong-Ansah, 1991, Rimmer, 1990).

Lt. General Akwasi Amankwa Afrifa replaced General Joseph Arthur Ankrah as chairman of NLC on April 2, 1969. In the general elections held soon thereafter, on August 29, 1969, the Progress Party led by Dr. Kofi Abrefa Busia won a landslide victory. Despite the NLC's attempt at improving Ghana's economy (and its external payments position in particular) by the time it handed over power to the Busia government there were still fundamental problems in the economy, such as an overvalued currency and fiscal deficits (see Table 1.1).

THE BUSIA GOVERNMENT

Like the NLC before it, the economic strategy of the Busia government was one of increased liberalization in trade and exchange regime. But unlike the NLC, which stressed economic stabilization, the Busia government emphasized economic growth through investment (Herbst, 1993: 22–24).[16]

The objectives of the Busia economic program were:

1. Raise domestic investment and savings;
2. Expand export earnings and attract more external assistance;
3. Accelerate the Ghanaianization of economic activities
4. Promote rural development (Killick, 1978: 57)

To further these economic goals, Busia, in July 1970, passed the Ghanaian Business Act, which amongst other things, established a credit-guarantee scheme to help Ghanaian businessmen. Furthermore, the Act set up the Office for Business Promotion with the sole purpose of assisting Ghanaians in business ventures. That same year, the Busia government dismissed 568 civil servants and abolished the Trades Union Congress (TUC), all with the intent of eliminating "waste" and promoting efficiency in public sector employment.

By 1971 however, it had become apparent that the economic polices of Busia had not succeeded in turning the Ghanaian economy around. Indeed, in the two years between 1969 and 1971, the Busia government accumulated external debts that equaled that which Nkrumah incurred in his nine years as President. (Killick, 1978: 55–62).

The Busia government, in December 1971, approached the Fund for financial assistance. Upon the recommendation of the Fund, the Busia administration invited a group of Harvard Development Advisory Service (DAS) economists to take over the formulation and planning of economic policy at the Finance Ministry. (Libby, 1976).

On Dec. 27, 1971 the Busia Government complied with the International Monetary Fund recommendation that to correct the currency overvaluation and spur export competitiveness, the Cedi would have to be devalued by 48.6%, to $0.55 (or 0.450182 grams of fine gold), as against $0.98, since its previous devaluation from $1.40 in July 1967 had failed to produce the desired reduction of imports (Libby, 1976). This devaluation was accompanied by other measures, including a 25% raise in public sector wages. The immediate impact of the devaluation was a steep increase in consumer prices, with fixed income earners and users of imported inputs bearing the brunt of these increases (Leith, 1974).

Seventeen days after this massive devaluation, the Busia Government was overthrown in a bloodless coup led by Col. I. K. Acheampong. The nexus of the coup to the devaluation further deepened hostility amongst successive regimes to compliance with IMF conditionality, in particular currency devaluation. As Herbst (1993: 23) notes: "the coup coming so closely after the devaluation, had an enormous impact on later governments when they contemplated resorting to market mechanisms to address their foreign exchange shortages."

THE NATIONAL REDEMPTION COUNCIL/ SUPREME MILITARY COUNCIL YEARS: 1972–79

The Acheampong Government: 1972–1978

Col. I.K. Acheampong, and the other coup leaders formed the National Redemption Council (NRC), comprising military officers, the head of the police, and one civilian. The NRC's stated objective for the coup was 'to bring to an end the economic mismanagement' by the Busia Government. To this end, the NRC set out to reverse the fiscal and monetary policies of the Busia government.

Colonel Acheampong announced on February 4, 1972 that with effect from February 7, 1972, the Bank of Ghana would exchange the Cedi for $0.78 (constituting a revaluation by 42%), which, he claimed, would reduce prices to the level existing before Busia's devaluation of December 27, 1971. He also rescinded the 5% development levy, which Busia's government has enacted the year before.

And in a move designed to lessen the burden of Ghana's existing foreign debts, Colonel Acheampong unilaterally repudiated debts[17] amounting to $94 million, incurred in respect of contracts entered into with four British companies—Parkinson Howard Group, Seawork Ltd., Newport Shipbuilding, and Swan Hunter Richardson. He also repudiated $72 million of accrued interest on debts incurred up to February 1966 (the month in which ex-President Nkrumah was overthrown). Acheampong's rationale was that the debts in question were "tainted and vitiated with corruption, fraud or other illegality" (Acheampong, 1972). The NRC, then reexamined all debts incurred before 1966, and repaid only those which his government believed had been incurred under valid contracts, concluded without corruption, and proved to be technically and economically viable. (Frimpong-Ansah, 1991: 94–114) (Keesings, 1972).

Acheampong's NRC political economic worldview, like that of Nkrumah's government before it, sought an augmented role of the state in managing the economy. Elucidating on his regime's economic philosophy, Acheampong said the NRC would "use state power to capture the commanding heights of the economy and to control it in such a way that its development will not go to benefit only a few handfuls of well-placed Ghanaians." (West Africa, 1972: 781).

Acheampong's brand of statist development was also cloaked in nationalism. He promulgated several indigenization decrees, which led to the State's seizure of 55% of equity shares in foreign mining and timber businesses, 50% shares in the breweries, and 40% shares in foreign owned banking and insurance companies (Boafo-Arthur, 1989:148). By the end of the NRC era, Ghana had the second largest number of state enterprises in Africa, after Tanzania, and one of the largest civil services. At the same time, Acheampong launched a program of economic self-reliance dubbed Operation Feed Yourself (OFY) and Operation Feed Your Industries (OFI).

To offset the country's growing deficits and foreign exchange scarcity, the NRC resorted to a policy of printing money. For, Acheampong the Cedi, the local currency, was symbolic of the country's pride and economic independence, and thus he saw no need to devalue it. (Leith and Lofchie: 1993: 233). This move caused inflation to rocket to unprecedented levels, reaching 116.5% by the end of 1977 (see Table 1.1).

It came as no surprise that the NRC regime, given its propensity to flaunt economic conventions, had very cool relations with the IMF, and other donor agencies. The only one occasion when Acheampong's NRC turned to the Fund for financial help was during the world energy crisis of 1974, which lead to an increase in oil prices. Then, Ghana's dearth of foreign exchange and credit left the country without fuel. On June 11, 1975, the IMF announced that Ghana had made its first purchase under the oil facility,[18] of the equivalent of $38.6 million special drawing rights, in respect of its 1974 balance-of-payments deficit. (Keesings, 1972).

Akuffo's SMCII: July 1978-June 1979

On July 5, 1978, in a bloodless coup, the other SMC[19] officers forced Acheampong to resign, placing him under house arrest. Lieutenant General Frederick W.K. Akuffo, the chief of the defense staff, replaced Acheampong as the head of state and chairman of the SMCII. Akuffo's government lasted for barely a year.

Under prompting from the IMF, the Akuffo's government introduced a stabilization package in August 1978 financed by a stand-by credit of SDR 53 million (Kessings, 1978, Hutchful, 1985).

The stabilization measures that SMCII agreed to comply with included:

1. Devaluation of the cedi by 58% against the U.S. dollar (from \$1.00=1.15 cedis to \$1.00= 2.78 cedis),
2. Reduction of the overall planned budgetary deficit from 1.5 billion cedis to 500 million cedis,
3. Increase in cocoa price from 40 cedis to 80 cedis per load,
4. Demonetization exercise to absorb the excess liquidity in the economy
5. Relaxation on the enforcement of price controls[20] (Jonah, 1988: 105–106)

Commenting on the stabilization package, the IMF announced on January 10, 1979 that the program aimed to reduce the rate of inflation by about one-half by September 1979 from the 100–125% that prevailed during the 12 months ended June 1978 and to correct price distortions, strengthen Ghana's balance of payments, and lay the basis for sustained growth of production and exports (Keesings, 1979). The IMF further announced on Feb. 15, 1979, that it had approved an interim disbursement to Ghana equivalent to SDR \$11.1 million from its Trust Fund for developing countries.

Most of these stabilization measures were not implemented as the country was reeling from mass protests and strikes. The SMCII in 1978 for example, had to declare a two-month state of emergency to contain striking workers (Chazan, 1988: 110).

In the environment of social unrest and strife, a group of junior and noncommissioned officers—the Armed Forces Revolutionary Council (AFRC), with Flt. Lt. Jerry John Rawlings as its chairman—deposed General Akuffo's government in a violent coup on June 4, 1979. (Schillings, 1982).

Rawlings' Armed Forces Revolutionary Council (AFRC): June 1979–September 1979

Rawlings and his 15-member AFRC pledged to allow the parliamentary and presidential elections to proceed as scheduled, on June 18, 1979. He announced however that the handing over of power to the victorious party would be delayed for three months, to October 1, 1979, to enable the AFRC to "complete its task of house cleaning." (Jeffries, 1989: 84–86), (Chazan, 1983).

Rawlings it seems was more intent on appealing to the masses for some form of moral reform, to halt exploitation, corruption, and *Kalabule* activity,[21] than on pursuing transformative macroeconomic reform (Aryeetey et al, 2000: 40). During his brief tenure (nearly four months) in office, Rawlings' regime enforced price controls, meted out severe, and sometimes publicly humiliating, punishment to "exploiters," and executed eight senior military officers, including three former heads of state—Afrifa, Acheampong and Akuffo—all for allegedly pilfering the nation's coffers. Not surprisingly, the Rawlings coup in effect halted the IMF stabilization measures initiated by the Akuffo regime.

Limann's People's National Party: September 1979-December 1981

On July 8, 1979, the CPP-inspired People's National Party (PNP), led by Dr. Hilla Limann, won the elections. The AFRC handed over power to Dr. Hilla Limann on September 24, 1979, (a week earlier than planned) but with much admonishment and warning on the need for the Limann's government to uphold the virtues and tenets of the AFRC "revolution," and "never lose sight of the new consciousness of the Ghanaian people" (Quoted in Nugent, 1995. p.79).

The Limann Government assumed office at a time when the state of the Ghanaian economy was precarious; characterized particularly by a severe foreign exchange shortage and a wide disparity between the official and "parallel" unofficial exchange rates of the Cedi. The fall in the internal value of the currency has been so rapid that by this period the Cedi valued only one-tenth of its 1971 purchasing power (Huq, 1989: 4). The over-valued Cedi in turn exacerbated the distortions in the economy and created ideal conditions for corruption, smuggling and a robust black market.

To remedy this situation the Limann Government undertook three main initiatives. First, it attempted to generate revenue, by introducing new taxes and reducing government expenditure. Second, it launched a new investment code in the hopes of attracting foreign investment. Third, it sought to garner loans and foreign aid from The Fund, and other donor communities, to finance urgently needed imports (Chazan, 1983: 311–320). However, as Naomi Chazan has noted, "The Limann regime's proposals [to address economic decline] offered palliatives where more [bold] moves were required." (Chazan, 1983: 313).

From January 21 through February 2, 1980, the Limann government and the IMF held their first meeting in Accra to discuss the terms and conditions under which the Limann government could borrow from the Fund. During this meeting the IMF offered the Limann government credits totaling $400 million (three-quarters of which would be in the form of a one-year standby credit and the remainder in the form of compensatory financing to offset an export decline due partly to falling world cocoa prices) in exchange for compliance with following measures:

1. an increase in the official prices paid to cocoa producers (who could obtain far higher prices by smuggling their crop to neighboring countries);

2. large increases in petrol prices (which were subsidized by the Government);
3. substantial reductions in government disbursement (major factors in which were the employment of some 300,000 civil servants and the existence of over 100 parastatal organizations);
4. a phased currency devaluation with the aim of bringing the official exchange rate closer to the unofficial rate.[22]

Dr. Limann was ready to go along with most of the policy conditions of the Fund but balked at the IMF's insistence of a currency devaluation out of fear that this would lead to a coup, as happened when Dr. Kofi Busia's government devalued the currency in 1971. Indeed, as Eboe Hutchful reminds us "the three highly unpopular devaluation's (in 1966, 1971, and 1978) made 'IMF' the most hated word in the Ghanaian political lexicon" at the time. (Hutchful, 2002: 13)

Ghana, Dr. Limann argued, was not "faced with the threat of any imminent economic earthquake that could warrant (the) government rushing into the political disaster of devaluing the Cedi."[23] Limann reasoned, instead, that aid must come before devaluation. He said: "first it was necessary to restock the country so that production could be revived and that then monetary steps could be taken progressively."[24]

Limann's inability to take bold economic reforms resulted in a steep decline in the economy, during the latter part of his period of office. Inflation rose to 116.5%, the highest since 1977 (see Table 1.1), and Ghana's balance of payments declined from a surplus of nearly $200 million in November 1980, to a deficit of $3 million by the end of November 1981 (in both cases, taking no account of arrears on current payments).[25] Per capita income, which had been approximately 640 Cedis in 1971, had declined by the end of 1981 to approximately 460 Cedis in constant (1975) terms. (Herbst, 1993: 27).

In the wake of the Limann government's indecision and hesitation to comply with the IMF stabilization package, Flight Lieutenant Jerry Rawlings, on December 31, 1981 overthrew that government—Ghana's fifth coup in 25 years!

CONCLUDING ANALYSIS OF THE HISTORICAL PATTERN

The relationship between the IMF and Ghana (prior to Rawlings' second coming) shows that in periods of economic boon, the political attitudes and ideological beliefs of the Ghanaian government's tend to be nationalistic (as in the Nkrumah, Acheampong, and Limann regimes), and its relationship with the IMF has been characterized by noncompliance. In other words, the political calculus of compliance with IMF conditionality was bound with charges of "neocolonialism." David Anaglatey captured this sentiment when he said,

> "It is as if the IMF is some sadistic monster which becomes angry at seeing people happy. . . . One also recalls with pride how Ghana's own Osagyefo [Kwame Nkrumah] rejected the Fund's pressures to devalue the cedi in the early 1960's. . . . Unfortunately many of the leaders Ghana has had after Nkrumah have not had the courage of the Osegyefo . They spinelessly yield to the IMF pressure."[26]

A second pattern is that the decision to comply with the IMF conditionality, in particular the use of exchange rate as an active policy instrument, had perceived political consequences, with leadership fears of a coup. Commenting on this prevailing psychology, Dr. Joseph Abbey said:

> "Procrastination of successive governments over a prolonged period in refusing to adopt appropriate stabilisation policies destroyed the country's economy, given the widespread belief that a stabilisation policy, especially devaluation of the exchange rate inevitably conjured up threats of a coup in Ghana. Consequently a succession of governments had held out until the bitter end before attempting any sort of stabilisation policy, so that economic conditions were particularly bad when they finally did make policy changes." (Abbey, 1987: 4)

Similarly, Boafo-Arthur, (1999: 22) noted that "Rawlings' predecessors either went to the IMF and lost political power, or for fear of losing power refused to accept IMF conditionalities but ended losing power all the same" (Boafo-Arthur, 1999: 22).

RAWLINGS' PROVISIONAL NATIONAL DEFENSE COUNCIL (PNDC)

On assuming power after the overthrow of Limann's PNP, Rawlings' PNDC was faced with the impending economic collapse. Inflation was running at 116%, the currency was seriously overvalued (see Table 1.1), and production in virtually all sectors had fallen by over 30% (Herbst, 1993: 27). The PNDC's policy responses (prior to seeking assistance from the IMF, in April 1983) were reminiscent of the AFRC period. The initiatives were initially based on ad hoc populist mobilization directed at achieving short-term stabilization, self-sufficiency and self-reliance. Later, a nationalist and anti-imperialist strategy of economic transformation was attempted.

January 1982-April 1983

In a televised address to the nation on January 5, Rawlings asked Ghanaians to "restructure the society in a real and meaningful democratic manner so as to ensure the involvement and active participation of [all] people in the decision-making process."[27] He declared a "Holy War" on corruption and announced the creation of a National Economic Review Committee (NERC) to review the country's economic condition and come up with recommendations on how to revive the economic infrastructure, though he offered no economic philosophy or package of his own.

Prior to the completion of the NERC report, in May 1982, the PNDC (as in the AFRC era) focused on stamping out corruption through the blatant use of force and populist mobilization (usually in the language of anti-imperialism and dependency thinking). Herbst notes that "with a flourish of populist and socialist rhetoric, the government sought to mobilize workers, students, and the rest of the urban population to bring about (through unspecified policy measures) radical change in the economy (1993: 28).

To the PNDC, the economic mess had a direct link with external capital. The preamble to policy guidelines of the PNDC attributed the decline in the economy to the local "comprador bourgeois" and "neo-colonialism," and thus the PNDC policies "must be anti-imperialist, anti-neocolonialist and must aim at instituting a popular democracy."[28] And the answer to the economic malaise of the country, the PNDC believed, lay in a state-directed control of its economic destiny. (PNDC, 1982). Further evidence of how dependency thinking influenced the early policies of the PNDC is obtained from a confidential government document entitled "Policy Guidelines For Ministries and Regional Organizations" released in May 1982:

> We must make a preliminary admission that Ghana today is a neocolony. . . . So we should commit the 31 December Revolution to the direct task of achieving economic independence by ensuring a fundamental break from the existing neo-colonial relations. In pursuit of this objective, we must commit this initial stage of the revolution to the national democratic struggle.

On the same page it elaborates further:

> The aim of this transformation must be first and foremost to break the existing foreign monopoly control over the economy and the social life. We must restructure the country along nationalistic lines to lead us into economic self-sufficiency, self-dependency and genuine economic independence.[29]

The PNDC from January through April 1983, when it accepted the IMF stabilization package, undertook several initiatives aimed at short-term economic stabilization. First it sought to slow down monetary expansion: The PNDC recalled and demonetized the 50 cedi bank notes (the highest denomination of the currency at the time); 1.3 billion cedis out of a total outstanding 50 cedi notes of 1.5 billion cedis was withdrawn from the public. The Government utilized the 1.3 billion cedis for debt retirement at the central bank. On a net basis, government outstanding debt to the banking system during the first half of 1982 was reduced by 643 million cedis.

Other measures introduced by the Government included: (a) the blocking and investigation of all deposit accounts in excess of 50,000 cedis ($1,500 at the time); (b) the introduction of compulsory payment by check for all business transactions in excess of 1,000 cedis; (c) the introduction, with the 1982/83 cocoa marketing season, of a system of payment to farmers by check instead of the traditional cash; (d) a temporary recall of personal bank loans for financing trading inventories; (e) the reduction in the structure of interest rates by about half (e.g., the maximum lending rate was reduced from 25.5% to 14% per annum, and the savings deposit rate was reduced from 18% to 8% per annum) (Gyimah-Boadi, 1986: 630–631).

NATIONAL ECONOMIC REVIEW COMMITTEE (NERC)

The first comprehensive economic package by the PNDC was the NERC report at the end of May 1982 in the form of a revised budget for the 1981–82 fiscal year. (The original budget for the 1981–82 fiscal year was drawn up by the deposed PNP government).

The NERC, as noted earlier, was established in January 1982, and comprised of technocrats who had served under previous regimes. Prominent among them were Dr. Joe Abbey, an economist who had been financial advisor to Generals Acheampong and Akuffo, Dr. Ato Ahwoi, Dr. Abudu and Dr. Erbynn both economists, and Mr. Kwesi Amoako-Atta (who had been Nkrumah's Finance Minister), Dr. Kwesi Botchwey, and the governor of the central bank, Dr. J. S. Addo, also became members.[30]

The NERC concluded that the ad hoc populist mobilization measures being carried by the Government was wrong-headed, and that the Government had no choice but to embark on stabilization and adjustment policies with assistance from the IFIs (Kraus, 1991: 124–125).

The NERC then proposed specific policies they believed would attract assistance from the IMF, the World Bank and the OECD countries. These measures included:

1. devaluation of the cedi to eliminate price distortions and provide incentives to exporters;
2. phasing out of price controls to eliminate speculation and hoarding by traders;
3. increases in producer prices of cocoa;
4. reductions in the size of the budget deficit; and
5. the elimination or reduction of some government subsidies. (Kraus, 1991: 124–125)

The NERC proposals, however, were rejected by influential elements in the PNDC that were opposed to any compliance with IFI conditionalities, particularly on the issue of devaluation. (Kraus, op.cit: 120–121)[31]

THE PROGRAMME FOR RECONSTRUCTION AND DEVELOPMENT (PFRD)

With the rejection of the NERC proposals, the PNDC continued to pursue its ad hoc economic policies (outlined above) until it unveiled its second statement of a comprehensive macroeconomic package, the Programme for Reconstruction and Development (PFRD), on December 30 1982.

The PFRD, a 48-page document, was announced in a televised broadcast by the Secretary for Finance, Kwesi Botchwey. The broad objectives of this four year program (1983–87) was intended to lay the foundations of a nationalist and anti-imperialist strategy of economic reconstruction and aimed:

1. to restore incentives for production of food, industrial raw materials and export commodities and thereby increase their output to modest but realistic levels;
2. to increase the availability of essential consumer goods and improve the distribution system;
3. to increase the overall availability of foreign exchange in the country, improve its allocation mechanisms and channel it into selected high priority activities;
4. to lower the rate of inflation by pursuing prudent fiscal, monetary and trade policies;
5. to rehabilitate the physical infrastructure of the country in support of directly productive activities;
6. to undertake major systematic analyses and studies leading towards a major restructuring of the economic institutions in the country.[32]

The PFRD envisaged a large and prominent role for the state. A state monopoly was to be established over import and export trade and the state's share in banking was to be increased from 40 to 80%. With respect to the IFIs, external finance and devaluation of the local currency, the PFRD gave no indication of changing the status quo. Herbst (1993: 28) notes that the PFRD "devoted itself to establishing a state monopoly on export-import trade, eliminating corruption in the allocation of import licenses, and trying to reorient trade away from the West." (emphasis added). According to Botchwey, the objective of creating state monopolies in the export-import trade sectors was to restrain the drain on foreign exchange resources through over-invoicing of imports and through transfers by foreign controlled commercial banks.[33]

Four months after the announcement of the PFRD, in April 1983, the PNDC in a stunning reversal of economic policy announced that it had accepted an IMF stabilization package and was willing to comply with its terms.

Why did Rawlings' PNDC go to the IMF despite its earlier radical populist strategy; what was the history of lending arrangements between the PNDC and the IMF; what were the objectives of the adjustment program; and how can one characterize the regime's overall relationship with the IMF? It is to these questions that we now turn.

NEGOTIATING ADJUSTMENT: THE IMF & GHANA, 1982–1983[34]

The PNDC abandoned its radical populism and approached the IMF, and other "financial imperialists" (Ahiakpor, 1985), for two main, overlapping, reasons. First, the economy had reached its nadir by 1983. The Ghana economy had by 1983 reached an all time low since the early 1970s. GNP per capita in 1983 (at 1975 constant prices) was 39% lower than 10 years earlier and 21.3% lower than in 1980. Food self-sufficiency had declined from 71% in 1973/80 to only 23% in 1982.[35] Export volume was only about half of its level in the mid 1970s while cocoa production was about 40% of its level in the mid 1970s. Mining and Manufacturing production had fallen by 1983 to about 50% and 40% respectively of the mid 1970 levels. Government revenue as a percentage of GDP had plummeted from 17.2% in 1974 to only 5.9% in 1981. The gross capital formation rate had also sunk to 7.3% of GDP by 1983, a little more than half the level of 1970. As can be seen from Table 2.1 the GNP per capita declined at the annual rate of 4.4% from 1973–1983, industrial output declined by 6% per annum over the same period, agricultural output per capita declined by about 3% per annum, exports declined by 6.4% and imports declined annually at 8% and the terms of trade fell 6.5%, while cocoa production dropped by 7.1% annually. Food production per capita declined at 5.9%, while inflation as measured by consumer prices galloped at about 50% annually over the 1973–1983 decade.[36]

To make matters worse, the country witnessed one of its worse national disasters, evidenced in the form of bush fires and severe droughts. Still, an estimated one million Ghanaians working in Nigeria were affected by a Nigerian Government announcement on Jan. 17, 1983, ordering the deportation of all illegal aliens. These repatriations, representing a 10% increase in the Ghanaian population (Tsikata, 1999:18) caused an immediate social and economic strain in the, already ailing, Ghanaian economy. To say the least, these factors exacerbated the fiscal crisis the country was facing at the time. The observation by M. Huq provides a valuable perspective on the economic crisis, one worth quoting: "The average Ghanaian in 1982 was much worse off than she was [at independence] in 1957." (Huq, 1989: 2).

In highlighting the role of Ghana's domestic crisis, we are in no way implying that crisis inevitably leads, or should lead, to compliance with IFI inspired reform. Williamson and Haggard, after surveying 13 countries, drew our attention to the fact that "crisis is clearly neither a necessary nor a sufficient condition to initiate reform."[37] However, in the case of Ghana, the dire economic conditions (cited above), no doubt, influenced the decision to talk to, and ultimately comply with, the Fund. This is evident in the thinking of Rawlings himself when he said:

> By December 31, 1981, our estimated disposable resources available for imports stood at about $33m. As against this, our outstanding short-term commitments stood about $348m. It is clear from this alone that we were facing bankruptcy . . . the estimated disposable resources were hardly sufficient to cover two week's imports.[38]

Again, he captured the gloomy economic picture and the need for sound economic action when on a national broadcast he further noted that:

> The cancer had reached a very advanced stage . . . when in the first quarter alone of 1981–82 financial year, the projected deficit for the whole year was almost being reached, it was quite clear that we were on a course of self-destruction. Not to apply the brakes and put us back on course would have been foolish.[39]

In short, it had become clear to the PNDC leadership, at least to its Chairman—Rawlings, that maintaining social control through the gun, without attempting to solve bread and butter issues, would not advance their "revolution."[40]

Table 2.1. Average Annual Growth Rates of Selected Basic Indicators

Indicator		**1965–73**	**1973–83**
1. Population		2.2	3.1
2. Domestic production			
(a)	GDP	3.4	-1.3
(b)	GDP per capita	1.2	-4.4
(c)	Agriculture	4.5	0.0
(d)	Industry	4.3	-7.0
(e)	Services	1.1	-0.3
3. Merchandise trade			
(a)	Exports	3.5	-6.4
(b)	Imports	-3.3	-8.0
(c)	Terms of trade	—	-6.5
4. Cocoa production		-1.2	-7.1
5. Food sector			
(a)	Food production	2.0	-2.7
(b)	Food production per capita	-0.3	-5.9
(c)	Calorie availability per Capita	1.3	-3.9
(i)	from cereals	3.8	-3.3
(ii)	from roots and tubers	-2.0	-1.8
(d)	protein availability per capita	4.1	-4.0
6. Inflation			
(a)	Consumer prices	6.3	49.9
(b)	Food prices (local and imported)	6.6	53.2
(c)	Non-food prices	5.8	46.5

Source: A Tabatabai Adjustment Policies and Access to food in Ghana, International Labor Review ILO Geneva, Vol. 127, No.6, p. 706.

The second reason the PNDC turned to the IMF is that it saw no plausible alternatives to international finance and capital. In particular, its flirtation with the Left for economic ideas and financial resources turned up empty (more on the turn to the Left immediately follows).

COURTING THE LEFT

The initial support base[41] of the PNDC consisted of an alliance between the military (the lower ranks in particular) and civilians on the political and ideological left (comprising a small section of the student body, radical elements in the trade union movement, left wing academics, and the urban unemployed) (Chazan, 1988: 115–116; Hutchful, 1989). Of this alliance the most influential, as far as economic ideas and policy was concerned, was the June Fourth Movement (JFM) and the New Democratic Movement (NDM).

The June Fourth Movement (JFM), originally under the chairmanship of Rawlings, and later Chris Atim (an initial PNDC member), was set up during the PNP regime to defend the aims and principles of Rawlings' June 4, 1979 (AFRC) revolutionary coup, and to create a socialist democracy in Ghana. Its membership was drawn from mainly students, workers and soldiers. (Ray, 1986: 47). The New Democratic Movement (NDM) was created in May 1980 with membership drawn from left wing intellectuals from the University of Ghana, professionals and urban civil servants. Like the JFM, NDM subscribed to some variant of Marxism. The main difference between the youthful JFM (in terms of the membership) and the older NDM was on what constituted the most effective strategy to achieving the goal of transforming Ghana into a socialist state. For the NDM leadership, true socialism could not be achieved until the right socioeconomic conditions were in place. The NDM argued that, putting the right socioeconomic infrastructure in place during the transition to socialism might necessitate collaboration (though undesirable) with international capital. As Kwesi Botchwey, the Finance Minister and former NDM member would later argue: agreement with the Fund was not a "sell out" but a necessary path that would "create as much space as possible" for the "revolution."[42] The JFM, on the other hand, rejected any association with international capital. Speaking of the twin Bretton Woods institutions, the JFM argued that the World Bank is "the master of the IMF" and the IMF is "the mercenary headquarters of imperialist companies, whose main aims are to ensure the continued exploitation and oppression of our people."[43]

For most of 1982, the JFM and the NDM vied for influence in determining the PNDC's economic policy, with the JFM gaining the upper hand for a better part of that period. This is because unlike the NDM, the JFM had members on the PNDC. Indeed, all the six original PNDC members other than Rawlings had direct ties with the AFRC, the JFM, or both.

Given the predominant influence of these left wing groups, particularly the JFM, the PNDC in the immediate aftermath of the coup aligned itself with the Socialist and Eastern countries.[44] The PNDC embarked on highly publicized aid-seeking missions to Cuba, Libya, USSR and Eastern European countries. During one such high-level delegation talks in the Soviet Union, a member of the PNDC (and a JFM founding member), Chris Atim, asserted that the true friends of Africa were socialist countries (Daily Graphic: November 20, 1982: 2). But as it turned out, an overwhelming majority of the Socialist bloc had economic difficulties of their own, and advised the PNDC to go to the IMF (Aryeetey et al, 2000: 44). As Zaya Yeebo, a JFM insider and former PNDC secretary, remarked, "I must admit that I was wrong—I thought we could go to the Soviet Union and the Scandinavian countries for help rather than the IMF. Only later did I realize that the Soviets were either unwilling or unable to help us."[45]

For the PNDC then, and like most adjusting country governments, it seemed all plausible alternatives to international finance and capital had evaporated (De Soto, 2000). In the PNDCs own words: "The analysis of both the historical development and the existing situation made it obvious that a large part of the resources necessary for investment to rehabilitate the productive and social infrastructure would have to be mobilized from external sources. In simple terms, we had to look quickly for financial help from the international community on a bilateral as well as multilateral basis" (Ghana, 1987: 3).

The turn to the intellectual Left for viable economic programs fared no better. After the Left rejected the NERC proposals in late May 1982, another committee was formed and charged with formulating a revised position on the economy that reconciled the complaints of Left (which equated compliance with IFI conditionalities to neocolonialism and further dependency) with the insistent demands by the technocrats (that IFI conditionalities were inevitable if the serious macroeconomic problems Ghana was facing were to be addressed). In the words of Hansen, compliance with IFI conditionalities, especially devaluation, became "the ideological and political construct around which battle lines were drawn" (1991: 106). To this end, the committee had two aims. First, it had to decide how much, if any, of the NERC's macroeconomic proposals it wanted to endorse, and second, it had to ensure that its economic proposals did not go against the socialist principles that it was committed to.

This committee, which was simply referred to as the "committee of the NDC and the PNDC secretaries on the economy," included members of the "progressive political organizations" Amoako Atta from the NERC and the NDM's Yao Graham. The likes of Samir Amin, Kwame Amoa[46] (from the Dakar based Institute for Planning and Development), Tetteh Kofi (from University of San Francisco–USA), and Eskor Toyo (from University of Calabar–Nigeria) were invited to Ghana to advise the committee on its work. Although these four advisors were not involved in drafting the final report they produced sectoral reports that were made available to all committee members (Hutchful, 2002: 51). Indeed, Graham credited these four advisors with enhancing the committee's understanding of the issues of political economy, something that "most people on the Left in Ghana had no idea about."[47]

On September 10, 1982, the committee presented its report (which some called the Alternative Development Program or the Graham Report) to the PNDC and the PNDC secretaries. The report (which was more of a framework than a detailed economic program), while it stressed economic self-reliance and a break from IFIs in particular and Western dependency in general, "offered no new sources of external capital" (Rothchild, 1991: 125). Indeed, the committee vaguely advocated dialogue with the IMF and argued strongly in favor of devaluation.

Given the fact that the issue of devaluation had prevented the PNDC initially from considering talks with IFIs, the committee's position on devaluation was indeed a coup for the technocrats. The committee's conclusions on devaluation are reproduced below:

- There is no doubt that the Cedi is grossly overvalued, judged by its black market value.
- This overvaluation leads to heavy smuggling.
- It also leads to the fact that export producers are hard put to it to cover their costs of production with the Cedi yields of their foreign exchange earnings.
- Price and financial irrationality has never helped any economy. It only leads to [in]stability and ruin.
- The Cedi will have to be devalued.
- The new rate has to be thoroughly realistic. It is useless fixing a Dollar-Cedi rate of 1:10, for instance, if the actual situation is that only 1:30 can correct the imbalances. There are, after all, countries, which have simply allowed their currencies to float.
- Our thinking in this matter is completely independent of any consideration of dealing with the International Monetary Fund. If the restoration of financial and price rationality will induce the IMF to come to the aid of revolutionary Ghana, all well and good: this

possibility should be pursued. However, we have to do for ourselves what we [deem] necessary.[48]

Not surprisingly, the JFM denounced the committee report. In an editorial that appeared a week after the committee report in the Workers Banner, the JFM wrote that the IMF influenced the committee's report:

> The International Monetary Fund (IMF) has been quietly and subtly negotiating with the Government: Yes, for the past couple of weeks the IMF—this financial monster, the mercenary headquarters of imperialist monopoly companies—has been laying 'time bombs' under the 31st December [Revolution]—to squeeze our finances, sabotage the economy, destroy the revolution and thus ensure the continued exploitation and oppression of our people.[49]

The JFM, and others on the radical left, lacking a viable economic program of their own and fearing that an agreement with the IMF was imminent tried unsuccessfully to topple Rawlings in October and November 1982. The failed coups by the radical Left was certainly a psychological tipping point for Rawlings, who by this time, was becoming convinced of bankruptcy of the Left and the economic necessity of an agreement with the IMF. On the limitations the self-reliant strategy advocated by the Left, Rawlings notes:

> Ghana's engagement in the international capitalist system has in no small measure contributed to the country's present predicament . . . One tempting solution is the complete disengagement of the country's economy from the exploitative capitalist world order . . . while such a solution should be our ultimate aim, it is not a feasible option in the immediate future.[50]

Rawlings had also come to the conclusion that domestic factors, particularly the factors that had contributed to declines in production, had a role in the country's demise. Explaining why the SAP was adopted, Rawlings notes:

> An impartial and objective study of the economic facts show clearly that production has declined steadily since 1975. What we have been witnessing is a severe crisis of economic production, which has drastically affected our earnings of foreign exchange . . . Why has it become so profitable in this country to engage in trade instead of production?

> . . . The surest cure to our longstanding ailment as a nation is a set of policies that will stimulate production and at the same time discourage unproductive activity. [51]

For Richard Jeffries, the lack of plausible economic alternatives to the IFI stabilization program, as was exemplified in the Ghanaian case, is a testament to the bankruptcy of the dependencia approach to development. Jeffries wrote:

> This was not just an unfortunate failure of particular individuals. It is a more general failure of dependency theory that it commonly does not distinguish between relatively large economies with abundant resources, at one extreme, and small economies with few resources, like Ghana's, at the other. Self-reliance might be a practicable option, even if not a developmentally optimal one, in the former case. It remains to be shown what alternative there is to international trade if one wants to raise living standards much above subsistence level in the latter case. (Jeffries quoted in Rothchild, 1991: 164).

THE IMF NEGOTIATIONS: JULY 1982-APRIL 1983

It is an arduous task to accurately reconstruct the details of the negotiations during this period without access to the entire key confidential Fund documents, the actors involved with all sides in the talks, and the PNDC's preparatory documents. However, information gleaned from some confidential IMF draft letters of intent and from confidential interviews (conducted with a few people involved with the negotiations), as well as information from published sources gives us substantial insights into when the negotiations occurred and what the various positions and issues were.

The initial contacts and negotiations with the Fund, which began in July 1982, were mostly secret. This is because (and as discussed previously) there existed, both within and outside of the PNDC, intense opposition to any dealings with the Fund, which was widely seen as an imperialist and exploitative institution.[52]

In July 25–29, 1982, a Fund team visited Accra (Ghana's capital) at the invitation of NERC[53] (and with authorization from Rawlings). Kwesi Botchwey, the Finance Minister, headed Ghana's delegation to the IMF talks. The aim of these talks was to draw the outlines of an economic program that would enable Ghana to attract financial assistance from the IMF and to establish Ghana's creditworthiness internationally. Specifically, the negotiations centered on Ghana borrowing an amount of SDR200m under a Stand-by Arrangement (a decision of the IMF by which a member is assured that it will be able to make purchases (drawings) from the General Resources Account (GRA) up to a specified amount and during a specified period of time, usually one to two years, provided that the member observes the terms set out in the supporting arrangement), and a further SDR 100m under a Compensatory Financing Facility (a special IMF financing facility established to provide resources to members to cover shortfalls in export earnings and services receipts, as well as excesses in cereal import costs, that are temporary and arise from events beyond the members' control).

The negotiations with the IMF were protracted and difficult. Subsequent to the July 1982 meeting, Ghana's delegation met with Fund members in two three-week sessions before an agreement in principle was reached: in Toronto and Washington on September 2–22, 1982 and again in Washington on January 28 through February 18, 1983. The talks focused on exchange rate adjustments, monetary and fiscal policy and external debt management. The main sticking point (and one of the reasons for the talks' secrecy) was the issue of devaluing the country's grossly overvalued currency. The IMF insisted on an immediate and massive devaluation whilst the PNDC, noting negative political consequences of devaluation's in the past, argued for a gradual and partial devaluation (Martin, 1991: 237-239). The PNDC was able to win a concession in the form of multiple exchange rates as a transition to a formal and permanent devaluation (the IMF gave the PNDC a year to unify the exchange rate system). The multiple exchange rate, the PNDC argued, would help address the exchange rate problem while politically it would take steam out of opponents who saw outright devaluation as capitulation with IMF demands (Herbst, 1993: 44). Indeed when the PNDC announced the transitional, multiple exchange rate for the cedi it argued publicly that the currency was not being devalued when in fact it had. Mrs. Aanaa Enin, a PNDC member, for example, assured Ghanaians that "the government has not devalued the cedi but had rather readjusted it to meet the economic conditions of the times."[54]

On April 21, 1983, the PNDC in its budget statement launched its Economic Recovery Program, which in essence were measures discussed with the IMF staff in February of that year. The most far-reaching measure was the introduction of a transitional multiple exchange rate for the Cedi. The new exchange rate, which was based on a system of bonuses and surcharges applied by banks and other authorized foreign exchange dealers, resulted in two rates: $1= 23.75 cedis, and $1= 29.97 cedis (compared with the rate of $1= 2.75, which had been in effect since mid 1978).

The PNDC government, having demonstrated (through the April 1983 budget) its willingness to comply with the IMF package held consultation discussions with the Fund, on the use of Fund resources as stipulated in Article IV of the IMF Articles, and to conclude the discussions of the ERP, on May 1–25, 1983 in Accra. At this meeting the PNDC and the Fund staff discussed and agreed on the contents of a draft letter of intent. Typically the government's Letter of Intent (addressed to the Managing Director from the Ghana's Finance Minister and Governor of the Bank of Ghana) to the Fund describes the policies that it intends to implement in the context of its request for financial support from the IMF. The PNDC sent its Letter of Intent (dated July 7, 1983) to the Fund, which approved Ghana's loan request in August 1983.

CONCLUSION

Despite the fact that association with IMF or compliance with IMF conditionality had become a highly sensitive political issue in Ghana (beginning with the Nkrumah government), Rawlings understood that in order to retain political power he would have to halt or reverse the country's free falling economy. Ironically, his initial support base, the radical left, had a negative memory of Ghanaian compliance with IMF conditionality but had no concrete economic agenda. Faced with this dilemma, Rawlings abandoned his support base and embraced IMF reform. The issue of how he carried out the reform and how it impacted various social groups is the focus of the next chapter.

Chapter Three

The Political Logic of IMF Compliance and Its Initial Distributional Impact on Social Groups

> "[Reform] will strike at the powerful vested interests—rentiers and patrons whose opportunities come under threat as these measures bite. That such interests fight back to regain ascendancy is only to be expected, and the recovery efforts will only be sustained if their political patronage no longer provides the protection they received in the past. That is why the politics of stabilization is so often also the politics of destabilization, as a government determined to effect these transformations will face attempts to overthrow it. Ghana has had its full share of such destabilization efforts."
>
> —T. Tsikata [PNDC Official] (1990)

INTRODUCTION

This chapter focuses on the politics of adjustment as a determinant of compliance. There are three main objectives. First, to map out the various "stakeholders" in Ghana, who were affected by compliance with IMF conditionality. To do this I distinguish among different elites and their interests, and between elite and non-elite interests. Second, to examine the conditions under which the Fund's demands weighed upon different constituencies, and how the various groups manifested their pleasure or displeasure. Third, to analyze the political strategies and tactics used to enforce compliance with IMF conditionality.

I will argue that in the process of consolidating his power, Rawlings switched his earlier social and political base, made up primarily of workers, students, army ranks, and intellectual leftists, and embraced the

Ghanaian national elite. The national elite, I argue, was willing to be co-opted[1] because they were immediate beneficiaries of the adjustment program. Thus, the politics of adjustment in Ghana preserved the existing class configurations in the country, which was elite-driven and supported by foreign capital interests.

I also argue that regime survival, the suppression of potential class antagonism, and compliance with conditionality was importantly dependent on strategies of intimidation, coercion and co-optation.

This chapter is important because it not only establishes the nexus between elite/non-elite interests and compliance (and informs our understanding on how domestic political structures impact compliance with IMF conditionalities) but it also gives insights, into the state's role in the economy. Herbst, for example, observed that understanding the immediate political ramifications of structural adjustment is extremely crucial because the ensuing alienation of key constituencies may lead to noncompliance (Herbst, 1990: 952). He goes on to point out that "precisely because these economic reform programs represent a fundamental threat to the way African governments conduct politics, studying the process of change also opens an important window on the actual workings of the African state" (Herbst, 1993: 2).

It is important to state (as I did in Chapter 1) that this manuscript does not aim to quantify the effectiveness of IMF conditionality. As such the focus of our discussions in this chapter will be on what each group's (political and economic) stakes were in terms of economic reform or conditionalities, and how these stakes differed from group to group. We examine five social groups: the national elite, student body, army, labor and business interests. The research is based on a selective and illustrative, rather than a comprehensive review of the elite groups in Ghana. The analysis of each social group will be immediately followed by a description of the strategies used by the regime to ensure compliance and political sustainability (i.e., the ability to adhere to the reform program over a specified period of time).

THE GHANAIAN STATE, SOCIAL GROUPS AND IMF CONDITIONALITY

Economic policymaking in Ghana, like much of Africa, has been the exclusive domain of the state.[2] And due to the scarcity of economic assets, the Ghanaian state has become a resource in itself; where the ruling regimes use their monopoly control of public resources to ensure the allegiance of a wide array of client groups to it, as a way of guaranteeing its survival (Chazan 1983, 1988).

Which Ghanaian groups, then, are so dominant and powerful (disproportionate to their numbers) that ruling regime's find it imperative to make concessions to them, in order to ensure political tenure, and what are their interests?

THE NATIONAL ELITE

According to Larry Diamond, a dominant social group is one that "owns or controls the most productive assets, appropriates the bulk of the most valued consumption opportunities, and commands a sufficient monopoly over the means of coercion and legitimation to sustain politically this cumulative socio-economic preeminence."[3]

In Ghana, the dominant social groups (which we refer to in this manuscript as to the national elite) that have benefited from the 'consumptive power of the state,'[4] and for whom national economic policies have been designed and implemented (to afford a continuous flow of economic rents and other remunerative opportunities) are:[5]

1. top professionals in the arts and sciences (including lawyers)
2. top echelon of the military (colonels and above)
3. top and eminent persons in business and commerce (including large landowners and wealthy commercial farmers)
4. senior administrators in the public and civil service, including union leaders
5. senior journalists (especially at the editorial level)
6. senior members of the clergy
7. holders of government office (i.e. ministers and analogous positions)
8. senior politicians
9. important traditional rulers

Before we provide evidence to show how the policy-making of the state benefits this dominant minority, there needs to be some understanding of where the basis of this national elite's power lies and what its interests and ideology are.

The power and status of the Ghanaian national elite results from the fact that it makes the major decisions in the society. Its decisions are political in the sense that they have far-reaching consequences for all facets of society. That small minority groups of people make the important decisions of the society is the essence of classical elite theory.[6] The core of the elitist doctrine can be reduced to Gaetano Mosca's timeless assertion: There are two classes of people in all societies—the class which rules and the class which is ruled. (Mosca, 1939: 50) The Ghanaian case is confirmed by Ghana's former premier and sociologist, Kofi Busia. He noted that the Ghanaian elite have pre-eminence over others; have some degree of corporateness or group character; have some consciousness of the position they occupy within society; enjoy high status; and are considered immutable, in the sense that they exert influence over the allocation of societal values (Busia, 1956: 426–428).

But, what determines the status positions of the Ghanaian national elite, and from whence comes its relative power vis-à-vis other social groups? We maintain that the national elite's relative position of dominance arises not primarily over the control of the means of production (or economic basis), but more importantly is determined by its occupation of echelon and strategic positions in Ghana's economic and social structure. Our argument is paralleled in sociology by C. Wright Mills' study of the "power elite" (1956:4), where he proposes that the power of the elite is an outcome of the hierarchical positions they occupy in "the institutional landscape" of the society.

Affirming this argument, Richard Sklar, writing on class formation in Africa, concludes that class relations in Africa, at the end of the day, "are determined by relations of power, not production" (1979: 537). Similarly, Larry Diamond noted that it is the elite's "strategic locations in the structure of power" which enables it to feed off the national economic pie (1987: 577).[7] The basis of the Ghanaian national elite, then, is its ownership of, and/or control over, strategic productive assets that emanates from their corporatist networks, which they then reproduce for their immediate and future advantage.

But since in practically all-modern societies power is concentrated in the hands of a small group of people which takes care of day-to-day decision-making (Birch 2001, 186), how do we characterize and justify the existence of the Ghanaian national elite?

The chief marker denoting the existence of an elite is that it constitutes a cohesive, unitary and self-conscious group. These characteristics can be found in almost all elite definitions and theories. These main features of elite existence have become known as the three Cs (Meisel 1958, 361): group consciousness, coherence, conspiracy, the last-mentioned term meaning a common will for action rather than secret machinations (Parry 1969, 31–32).

There appears to be consensus that class consciousness and solidarity is present amongst the Ghana national elite. Max Assimeng, writing on the social structure of Ghana, concluded that the national elite, "in the sense of segments of the population who enjoy similar economic circumstances and life chances, and who wish to improve upon their position and to maintain a distance from those who do not belong to such positions, clearly exists in Ghana" (Assimeng, 1981: 123).

But what unites the Ghanaian national elite and what are their interests? Analysis on the Ghanaian national elite point to the same conclusion: the national elite do have, and share, a commonality of material and ideological interests that is decidedly pro-western. These interests are reflected in elite attitudes of (a) the 'national self' and (b) political and social organization of the society. Writing on the Ghanaian national elite, Ofuatey Kodjoe (1985) found that the national elite[8] has similar economic motivation because they have similar economic opportunities. He concluded that the Ghanaian national elite have "a strong commitment to liberal/conservative ideologies, characterized mainly by a preference for laissez-faire economics capitalist development, liberal democratic politics tinged with elitism and a modernizing ethic based on the emulation of 'western' way of life" (1985: 60). Explaining the proclivity of the national elite to western way of life, Paul Harrison (1979: 53) noted that "the departure of the colonial powers had created a status vacuum the filling of which gave a further boost of Westernization. The old sources of status in ceremony, ritual and traditional power were dying. The new power strata, politicians, bureaucrats and businessmen, sought to define their status against each other by the only method all of them recognized; flaunting of material goods of a western kind." The operational premise underlying studies like these is the proposition that Max Assimeng put best: "even if the present class structure of the Ghanaian society is not patterned on the model of American and European industrialized society, it may be assumed that it will in the course of time come to be so" (Assimeng, 1981: 123–124).

We shall now detail three policies and budget allocations (administrative and civil service wages, parastatal policy and social spending) to provide evidence to our claim that the structure and practice of economic policy-making in Ghana has had a skewed distributional impact toward the national elite.[9]

A. Illustration: Government expenditure for administration and wages

Table 3.1 reveals that general government expenditures for 'administration'—the wages and salaries of state personnel—is, on average, three times as much what was spent on all community services (including roads, fire prevention, water and sanitation) between 1976 and 1989.

Similarly, Table 3.2 demonstrates that civil servants, less than 15% of the population, absorbed an average of 30% of the government expenditure (in the form of wages and salaries) between 1975 and 1989, twice the amount of money absorbed for capital expenditure over the same period.

Table 3.1: Recurrent Expenditures, 1976–1989
(Millions of Cedis)

ITEM	1976/ 1977	1977/ 1978	1978/ 1979	1979/ 1980	1980/ 1981	1981/ 1982	1982	1983	1984	1985	1986	1987	1988	1989
A. General Services:														
General Administration	173	315	412	490	1248	965	1285	2829	4016	7382	7930	6792	14942	16163
Defense	80	129	175	125	332	490	439	648	1459	2664	3795	4275	4461	4959
Justice and Police	68	126	151	186	245	320	326	531	1149	2570	3833	6117	8358	9233
Sub-Total:	326	570	738	800	1824	1775	2049	4008	6623	12616	15558	17183	27761	30355
B. Community Services:														
Roads and Waterways	20	42	53	81	90	132	123	178	423	376	616	1720	2501	2669
Fire Protection, Water & Sanitation	13	23	122	242	377	-	-	-	-	-				
Other Community Services	16	36	64	45	124	83	74	246	516	631	1009	2245	1947	3293
Sub-Total:	49	101	239	363	590	214	197	424	939	1007	1625	3965	4447	5962
C. Social Services:														
Education	314	553	846	965	1242	1696	1704	2883	5251	9803	16247	25358	34636	41394
Health	117	204	304	278	418	501	486	587	2112	3765	5407	7348	10760	16286
Social Security, Welfare	78	63	82	242	-7	316	738	618	1111	2204	3751	6445	9904	14253
Other Social Services	31	60	69	84	135	155	153	190	331	415	618	383	1070	1175
Sub-Total:	540	880	1300	1569	1788	2669	3081	4278	8805	16187	26023	39534	56370	73108

D. Economic Services:														
Agriculture & Non-Mineral Resources	126	344	390	487	680	803	828	1389	936	1276	2121	3469	3384	5642
Fuel and Power	1	6	2	2	2	3	3	19	33	33	43	14	12	13
Min. Resources, Manuf., Const.	28	51	55	82	98	101	104	213	488	531	932	1136	1141	1319
Transport, Storage, Comm.	18	47	69	78	103	100	99	211	301	621	1242	1194	1043	955
Other Economic Services	2	3	5	3	3	4	4	191	360	524	693	1186	1341	1581
Sub-Total:	174	450	520	652	886	1012	1037	2023	2118	2984	5031	6999	6921	9510
E. Unallocable Expenditure:														
Gen Transfer to Local Govt.	44	80	106	154	213	274	309	464	739	580	1256	2314	3543	1960
Other	177	242	514	726	1021	1973	2168	2204	3425	5086	11341	10587	11961	18744
Sub-Total:	220	321	620	880	1234	2247	2477	2668	4214	5666	12597		15504	20704
F. Statistical Discrepancy	-0	-0	-82	192	8	-0	812	164	627	1327	1420	1429	0	9004
Grand Total	1308	2322	3335	4077	6329	7917	8029	13564	23326	39787	62253	82010	111004	148643

Source: World Bank

Table 3.2. Central Government Expenditure and Net Lending, 1975–1989

	1975	1980	1981	1982–1983	1984	1985	1986	1987–1988	1989
	Economic Classification (In percent of total expenditure and net lending)								
Total expenditure	94.6	96.7	97.2	97.1	95.6	96.4	95.5	96.0	96.2
Current expenditure	75.1	82.2	89.4	84.9	80.3	83.0	75.3	74.1	72.8
Goods and services	50.2	48.4	47.9	56.9	57.4	57.5	56.5	56.7	54.8
Wages and salaries	30.1	28.5	24.7	19.2	30.3	35.7	33.6	33.0	30.8
Other goods and services	20.1	19.9	23.2	37.7	27.0	21.7	22.9	23.7	24.0
Interest payments	6.1	12.8	14.5	12.5	10.6	15.5	9.9	8.0	9.2
Subsidies and transfers	13.7	21.0	27.0	15.5	12.3	10.0	9.0	9.4	8.8
Capital expenditure	19.5	14.4	7.9	12.3	15.2	13.4	17.3	19.9	18.7
Special efficiency	–	–	–	–	–	–	2.8	2.0	4.7
Net lending	5.4	3.3	2.8	2.9	4.4	3.6	4.5	4.0	3.8
(In percent of GDP)									
Total expenditure	21.7	19.1	8.0	9.9	13.3	13.8	13.7	13.7	13.9
Current expenditure	17.2	16.3	7.4	8.6	11.2	11.9	10.8	10.6	10.5
Capital expenditure	4.5	2.9	0.6	1.2	2.1	1.9	2.5	2.7	2.7
Total expenditure and net lending	22.9	20.0	8.2	10.2	14.0	14.3	14.3	14.3	14.4
Memorandum items									
Capital expenditure (broad)	–	–	0.6	1.9	3.3	5.0	5.4	5.8	5.1

Total expenditure (broad)	–	–	8.2	11.1	15.4	19.2	19.1	18.9	18.9
Functional Classification (In percent of total central government expenditure)									
General public services	25.8	21.0	26.4	24.9	21.3	20.8	19.3	22.0	19.3
Defense	7.8	6.3	4.6	6.0	7.5	6.5	6.5	3.2	3.1
Education	20.6	17.1	20.4	20.2	18.0	23.9	23.9	25.7	24.3
Health	8.3	6.4	4.4	8.6	9.8	8.3	8.3	9.0	10.1
Social security and welfare	11.0	7.2	4.3	4.2	5.0	5.3	6.4	6.9	7.3
Housing and community amenities	–	–	1.7	2.1	2.0	1.9	1.9	3.5	2.6
Other community and social services	3.9	3.1	1.8	2.2	1.5	1.7	1.7	1.5	2.0
Economic services 2	16.2	22.7	21.6	18.9	23.8	15.4	18.6	17.9	16.9
Interest on public debt	6.5	13.2	14.9	12.8	11.1	16.1	10.4	8.3	9.5
Special efficiency	–	–	–	–	–	–	2.9	2.1	4.9

Source: IMF

1. Data for 1975 and 1980 are on a fiscal year basis (year ending March); from 1983 onward the fiscal year coincides with the calendar year.

2. Includes services for agriculture, forestry and fishing, mining, manufacturing and construction, roads, and other transport and communication.

B. Illustration: Parastatal policy

Despite their economic non-viability, State Owned and Operated Enterprises (SOE) flourished in post-colonial Africa. Prior to the PNDC's acceptance of IMF conditionality in 1983 Ghana had a total of 235 state enterprises of which the government had a majority holding in 181,[10] even though the available data suggested a negative rate of investment. For instance, between 1980 and 1982, the deficits of Ghana's SOEs were 0.2–3.3% of the GDP.[11] Why, then, were these SOEs supported despite their poor performance? Nafziger (1993: 50) argues that these SOEs were used by the African elite to further the patron-client relationships that form the base of its power, and that it is in so doing that these SOEs became bloated and inefficient. Ghana's State Fishing Corporation (SFC) provides a typical example of how SOEs became management tools of politicians: in its 27 years of existence, the SFC had as many as 18 Chief Executives. (West Africa, June 27, 1988, p. 1152). Also, several Commission, Committee and Auditor General's Reports, such as Report on Accounts of Ghana, Third Report for 1971 Public Boards and Corporations and The Justice Archer Committee Report on Ghana Cocoa Board 1975 found that ruling regimes used SOE's as a vehicle to reward party sympathizers and cronies.

C. Illustration: Social spending

It is instructive to note that even during compliance with IMF conditionality whatever social spending or government subsidies in place tend to disproportionately benefit the rich and the elite. A recent World Bank study on the incidence of public social expenditures in Ghana indicate that the poorest 20% of the population consumed only 12% of the total health subsidy, even as 33% went to the richest 20% (see Table 3.3). The same was true for subsidized education in 1992: the poorest quintiles consumed 16% of total education, while the richest 20% gained 21%.

Our argument that national budgets and economic policy have historically reflected the relative powers of national elite, rather than the broader public interest, does not mean that Ghana's drastic economic decay (detailed in Chapter 2) are consequently in the interest of the national elite. This is not necessarily so. What we are arguing is that the national elite is only interested in its self: it is less concerned with the overall economic development agenda of the state per se, and more concerned with how much of the national resources accrue to it. As the main beneficiaries of state income, the national elite selfishly absorbs expenditures that could otherwise have been used for national development (Diamond, 1987: 575). In other words, the national elite views the state, not as a vehicle for 'development' or as a way to serve the mass public, but rather as a vehicle to exploit the national

Table 3.3: The Incidence of Public Social Expenditures:

Comparative Statistics for Ghana and selected countries

	Health		Education	
	Poorest	Richest	Poorest	Richest
Country (date)	quintile	quintile	quintile	quintile
Ghana (1989)	12	31	17	24
Ghana (1992)	12	33	16	21
As compared to:				
Colombia (1992)	27	13	23	14
Malaysia (1989)	29	11	26	13

a. Percentage of total government spending on health and education.

Source: Demery, S. Chao, R. Bernier and K. Mehra, The Incidence of Social Spending in Ghana (Wash. D.C.: World Bank, unpublished, 1995).

treasury for its own benefit. 'Development,' should it occur, is inconsequential. Robert M. Price made this point best when he concluded:

> The Ghanaian state has acted as a mechanism for the distribution of economic resources to the myriad of groups and individuals that could make effective political claims on it. . . . Whatever the original developmental goals of Ghanaian state economic intervention, economic policy has been placed at the service of political ends. Consequently, economic resources have been transformed into largesse. The securing of political incumbency, not economic development, has been the operative goal of this mode of statist economic strategy.[12]

THE NATIONAL ELITE, IMF CONDITIONALITY AND DOMESTIC POLITICS

As shown in Chapter 2, the PNDC, when it assumed power in 1981, was against the elite establishment. In Rawlings' own words, his coup was necessary to punish "the military senior officers, all those politicians, all those business and foreign criminals who have used [Ghana's] blood, sweat and tears to enrich themselves."[13] Living up to the platform of *people's democracy* on which it came to power, the PNDC, in the first two years, sought to reduce the extensive clout that the national elite had over the political economy by (1) purposefully excluding the national elite from policymaking and (2) pursing populist economic policies. [14]

The initial composition of the PNDC is a good indicator of the exclusion of the national elite and the regime's social force alliance. When a few soldiers from the "Boys Company," (notably L/Corporal Gyiwa, Corporal Adabugah and Sergeant Aloga Akata Pore) wrestled power from the Limann government, the PNDC regime that replaced it had seven members. The seven members, in the order listed in the PNDC proclamation[15] were: Flt. Lt. Jerry John Rawlings (Chairman and Head of State); Brig. Joseph Nunno- Mensah (member and Chief of Defence Staff); Rev. Kwabena Damuah (Member)[16]; W.O. Class One Joseph Adjei Buadi (member and coordinator, Armed Forces Defence Committee); Sergeant Daniel Aloga Akata Pore (member and secretary Armed Forces Defence Committee); Joachim Amartey Kwei (member)[17]; and Chris Bukari Atim (member).

As indicated in previous chapter, the PNDC from January 1982 through April 1983, also implemented several radical populist economic measures, such as arbitrary and ruthless behavior toward business interests (Kraus, 2002: 398: 409); recall and demonetization of the 50 cedi bank notes (the highest denomination of the currency at the time); the blocking and investigation of all deposit accounts in excess of 50,000 cedis ($1,500 at the time); the introduction of compulsory payment by check for all business transactions in excess of 1,000 cedis; and the imposition of compulsory price controls to placate workers. (Gyimah-Boadi, 1986: 630–631).

However, a series of events in 1982 resulted in a shift in both ideology and the class basis of the regime, toward the national elite (Hansen 1982; Hutchful 1989; Haynes 1989).

First, (as outlined in Chapter 2) members of the regime and the social groups that gave it its initial support and legitimacy—the left-wing intellectuals, organized labor and the leadership of the Ghana Trades Union Congress (TUC), junior officers of the army, the National Union of Students (NUGS), and the People's Defence Committees (PDCs) and Worker's Defence Committees (WDCs)—although ideologically opposed to any dealings with the IMF,[18] were (as discussed in the previous chapter) unable to provide workable economic policy proposals, and were ultimately without an adequate base to support the regime (Hansen 1982).

Second, there was intense social conflict and power struggle amongst the regime leadership. As Yeebo explains "it became obvious that for any anti-IMF alternative to work, there needed to be a change of political leadership" since the PNDC leadership "was full of petty bourgeoisie radicals; people who had no real commitment to radical change" and who were willing to "go with the IMF and get what they wanted: power, influence, money."[19] The struggle within the regime on which path the 'revolution' should take resulted in several attempts at regime change. On October 28, 1982, some NDC members announced the overthrow of Rawlings as the chairman of the PNDC and his replacement by Sgt. Alolga Akata Pore and Chris Atim. Later, on November 23, 1982, an attempted coup d'etat, reportedly staged by followers of Sgt. Akata Pore, was crushed after fierce fighting around PNDC headquarters in Accra and the main army barracks at Burma Camp (also in Accra). A dusk-to-dawn curfew was imposed the following day, and Sgt. Akata Pore and six other soldiers were arrested 'pending investigations into their role of inciting troops to mutiny.' Mr. Chris Bukari-Atim, another PNDC member, went into exile in Togo after the failure of the November coup, and was dismissed from the PNDC on February 3, 1983. In a letter addressed to Rawlings, Chris Atim wrote, "I am appalled at the obvious betrayal of the revolutionary hopes and aspirations of our people which you are carrying out with monstrous cynicism under the banner of revolutionary rhetoric and barefaced lies" (quoted in Yeebo, 1989: 170). Finally, on December 16, 1982, the country's 20,000-man army was placed on high alert following reports of incursions by rebel soldiers based in Togo.[20]

Third, excesses by its initial support base in the name of 'revolution' started to create political problems for the regime. The kidnapping and murder of three senior High Court judges in June 1982, in which members of the PNDC regime were implicated, stands out. Indeed, one of the PNDC founding members, Amartei Kwei, widely believed to have been made a scapegoat, was subsequently convicted and executed for his role in the murders. This incident also had the effect of driving out many of the early supporters of the regime. According to Zaya Yeebo, he resigned as a PNDC minister because "the deteriorating human rights situation, especially after the murder of the judges, made [him] feel uneasy."[21] Further, isolated acts of vigilantism, carried out by social organizations linked to the regime, increased in frequency. These acts prompted the state-owned Daily Graphic to issue a statement of concern,[22] and forced Rawlings to make a public statement at a May Day rally condemning the activities of such Defense Committees.[23]

The response of the PNDC, or what remained of it, to these series of events was to purge the membership and political structures of all the leftist radicals. As Matthew Martin put it "Rawlings had an excuse to purge almost all anti-IMF government members by the end of 1983" (Martin, 1991: 241). Indeed, by the end of 1983, Rawlings was the only one of the original seven PNDC members to remain in office. The PNDC, by this time was composed of two soldiers (Flt-Lt. Jerry Rawlings (chairman); Warrant Officer Joseph Adjei Boadi); two technocrats (Ms. Aanaa Enin;[24] Mr. Ebo Tawiah);[25] and one conservative politician (Naa Folku Konku Tsiri).[26] Rawlings, further co-opted the conservative social groups and the old political center when he announced as part of "the first stage of an expansion programme," on July 16, 1984, the addition of a conservative notable (Mr. Justice Annan)[27] and ex-politician (Mrs. Suzanna Alhassan).[28]

By this time, it is not only PNDC membership that had changed to embrace the national elite but the PNDC cabinet itself, which now included traditional chiefs (Agogohene Nana and Lawyer Akuoko Sarpong and Agona Nsabahene Nana and Lawyer Oduadum), ex-politicians (J.Y. Jantuah and J.A. Kuffour), and notable intellectuals (such as Ama Atta Aidoo, Prof. Mawuse Dake, and Dr. Joe Abbey) to name a few.

Thus, by the end of 1983, Rawlings had not only changed his populist policies to adopt IMF-backed reforms but he had also changed his ruling personnel to reflect the establishment. According to Yeebo, "Jerry [Rawlings] needed a U-turn to convince the Ghanaian ruling class, and external forces that he was not a rabid radical, neither was he in the payroll of [rogue nations such as] Libya."[29]

The point to note is that Rawlings, lacking any firm ideological beliefs, was willing to align himself with IMF conditionalities and the national elite so long as it appeared consistent with his vision of transforming Ghana's socio-economic landscape.[30]

Despite their initial skepticism and coolness to the PNDC, the national elite threw their political backing behind the IMF reform for several reasons. First, the national elite was convinced of the redefinition of the regime's structures and relations of power away from the Left (Hutchful, 2002: 40–41). The change in orientation of the PNDC as evinced in its membership, the neutralization of the revolutionary organs, Rawlings' spirited defense of the IMF package, and his public chides and verbal attacks on the Left (he variously derided the Left as having only "empty theories,"[31] of "ideological slogan shouting,"[32] and of "populist nonsense."[33]) were enough to convince the national elite that the regime had abandoned its revolutionary credentials. It is worth emphasizing that the national elite, which bore the brunt of punishment, meted through the regime's initial revolutionary vehicles like 'people's courts/tribunals' (Panford, 1994: 76), were genuinely apprehensive of losing their economic and political power to the non-elite class (Ofuatey Kodjoe, 1998: 182). By embracing IMF conditionality, the national elite became nominally in charge of managing compliance; giving it (the national elite) the de facto power to become noncompliant under any politically opportune pretense, or when its class interests were threatened.

Second, and more important, the potential redistributive impact of IMF conditionality[34] benefited the status quo: national elite and foreign commercial interests. Below are a few examples. First, the government used the new credits it was securing from the international donors to support the rehabilitation of 'key sector' industries. A key sector industry was defined by the PNDC as one that (a) produced essential goods for domestic consumption; (b) generated significant government revenue; (c) generated substantial foreign exchange through export; and (d) generated considerable employment (Ninisin, 1991: 70). Second, the banking system dished out generous credit to the formal sector manufacturers. According to the Bank of Ghana, during the 1983–84 fiscal year, total credits by primary and secondary banks[35] to public (apart from the central government) and private sector bodies[36] increased by 4,269.5 million cedis or 88.3% to 9,104.5 million cedis at the end of the year, compared with a growth of 1,159.2 million cedis or 35.2% in the previous year. The manufacturing sector benefited the most, receiving an increase of 1,624.4 million cedis or 213.8% (Ninsin 1991: 68–72). If we also take into account the fact that the value of imports increased from 2,781.6 million cedis in 1982 to 69,881.0 million cedis in 1986 (Ninsin, 1991: 71) then the implications of this data become clear: only persons who had access to foreign capital or who were placed in strategic positions in these industries were able to take advantage of these credits.

Given the above evidence it is easy to agree with Yeebo when he says, "the elite who initially opposed Rawlings soon saw economic advantages, which SAP brought to them, and became ardent supporters of the government: Every economic policy has to benefit a certain section of the population, in the case of Jerry's [Rawlings'] reforms, they benefited foreign companies and the Ghanaian elite, especially, those with links to foreign companies."[37]

NON-ELITE GROUP INTERESTS AND IMF CONDITIONALITY

1. Labor

African labor unions have been variously described as apolitical, economistic, and as "organizations of the privileged" (Markovitz, 1977: 263–271; Bates, 1981; 1971).

Yet most agree that the labor's strategic location in the cities, especially the capital, gives them the potential power to disrupt and paralyze governments. Elaborating on the unique power of labor, Robert Bates said:

> direct attacks on labor movements are open to reprisals; in moments of economic stress, labor movements can join with their urban constituents, paralyze cities, and create the conditions under which ambitious rivals can displace those in power. And attempts at co-optation still leave open the chance for wildcat actions; during moments of economic crisis in the cities, workers can and have acted on their own" (Bates, 1981: 31).

Ofuatey Kodjoe emphasized this very point when he wrote that organized labor in Ghana was a special concern to the PNDC, "not only because they were capable of causing widespread political unrest, but also because they were strategically located to undermine the ERP, because of their pivotal role in the production process" (Ofuatey Kodjoe, 1998: 174)

There are however differences within the ranks of labor everywhere (Markovitz, 1977: 263) and the case of Ghana is no exception. Notwithstanding this fact, there are three main issues that are central to labor interests in Ghana.[38] First, Ghanaian labor has been a staunch advocates of two "core" International Labor Organization (ILO) principles: the right to freedom of association and the right to organize and to bargain collectively.[39] Ghana became a member of the ILO in 1957. Since then, Ghana's labor force has, on numerous occasions, exercised power through organized or spontaneous demonstrations to protest the state's encroachment of these rights. Commenting on the political nature of the Sekondi-Takoradi railway strikes of 1950, 1961 and 1971, Richard Jeffries observed that the strikes "were consciously directed against the government rather than the management, and were expressions of protest at general policies and characteristics of the regimes in question rather than narrowly occupational grievances."[40]

Second, labor aims at narrowing the wide disparities between civil service and private sector salaries, and to bridge the gap between income differentials generally by providing workers with a decent 'living wage.' As Kraus noted, labor strikes in Ghana between 1968 and 1971 was to "articulate the interests of the broadest stratum of labor, the lower-paid and minimum-wage earners."[41]

Third, labor seeks not only cordial relations with the political regimes but expects them to consult with labor in economic policy formulation and implementation. In 1965 (at labor urging), The National Labour Advisory Committee was set up by the Nkrumah government to institutionalize tripartism (a mechanism for social dialogue and partnership between representatives of labor, management and government) and consultations with labor (Panford, 1994: 91).

LABOR, IMF CONDITIONALITY AND DOMESTIC POLITICS

In its first two years, the PNDC positioned itself as a labor friendly regime and, in turn, enjoyed high political support from Ghana's Trades Union Congress (TUC), the umbrella group for labor in Ghana.[42] The PNDC was seen as representing labor interests in the following ways. First, it made executive decisions to directly placate labor. The PNDC started out by reinstating a group of workers fired by the previous regime and by taking a hard stance against the TUC leadership, who were seen by the labor rank as part of the Ghanaian aristocracy. As a gesture of concern, Rawlings' government on seizing power, reinstated 1,000 workers who had been dismissed from the Ghana Industrial Holding Corporation (GIHOC) during the Limann regime. Four months later, on May 25, 1982, Mr. Joshua Amartey Kwei, a PNDC member and former trade union activist, (who had been dismissed by the Limann government the previous year for organizing a strike at the GIHOC) announced the dismissal of the entire TUC leadership (which had been criticized as "bankrupt and undemocratic" by the ACLU) and appointed an interim management committee to handle union affairs and prepare for democratic elections to the TUC (Ninsin, 1987). In any event, the TUC leadership did not have credibility and the widespread support of its members because it had collaborated with successive regimes (Acheampong, Akuffo, Limann) at the expense of unionized workers (Jeffries, 1991: 161).[43] The PNDC capitalized on the TUC's legitimacy crisis by encouraging the formation of Workers Defence Committees (WDCs). The WDCs differed from the traditional unions, in three significant ways. First, in contrast to the traditional unions, which were for most part apolitical, focused mainly on economic issues in the strict sense, the WDCs openly entered into a political alliance with the PNDC and shared its revolutionary zeal and mission. The second point of difference between the unions and the WDCs was that the latter sought a direct democracy in the relations between workers and management, with workers being more in charge of their destiny, and better accountability from management. Third, the WDCs had no faith in the structures and organs of the union leadership and sincerely wanted alternative frameworks that would inform their roles and interests (Hutchful, 2002: 171). In sum, the WDCs operations seemed intent on supplanting, rather than complementing, the labor unions as instruments of worker's power (Graham, 1989: 44–52; Ninsin, 1989 and 1991).

The second reason workers supported the regime in its early phases was because the PNDC consulted regularly with labor, and the mass public, on national policy. The national budget, as an example, was publicly debated in open fora held at the Kwame Nkrumah Conference Center in

Accra during the regime's first two years, with active labor participation (Panford, 1994: 76).

Third, sections of the PNDC's 1982 'Directive Principles of State Policy' which laid out the framework for government policies was certainly pro-worker, if not pro-people. The principles enunciated called for:

1. a basis of social justice and equality of opportunities is to be established, with particular attention being paid to the deprived sections of the community, and to the reconstruction of society in a revolutionary process directed against the previous structures of injustice and exploitation;
2. respect for fundamental human rights and for the dignity of the human person are to be cultivated among all sections of the society and established as part of the basis of social justice;
3. the economy of the nation is to be managed in such a manner as to secure the maximum welfare, freedom and happiness of the people of Ghana, and to provide adequate means of livelihood and suitable employment to the members of the society, and public assistance to the needy;
4. educational facilities at all levels are to be provided and made available to the greatest extent possible, the paramount responsibility of the State for the provision of such facilities being acknowledged;
5. the health, safety and welfare of all persons in employment are to be safeguarded and the basis established for the full deployment of the creative potential of all within the society (Haynes 1991, 412).

A final reason why labor threw its weight behind the PNDC regime was because radical labor leader activists like Ebo Tawiah and Amartey Kwei, as well as other elements with labor sympathies, were members of the PNDC government or closely connected to Rawlings (Amankwah, 1990: 74).

However, when the government announced an agreement with the IMF and imposed the IMF conditionalities, workers withdrew their support, arguing that policies entailed in the conditionalities, such as privatization, devaluation and retrenchments, were anti-worker and anti-people. Emphasizing the position of worker betrayal at the implementation of IMF conditionality, Mr. A. K. Yankey, then the new head of the TUC, said: "The plain truth is that the ordinary Ghanaian, the poor worker, is suffering [as a result of IMF conditionalities]. And the government must know that there is a limit to human endurance."[44] He added further that "the government that said that the coup on 31 December was a revolution for the workers and the masses is now running the country like a business."[45]

IMF conditionality adversely impacted labor rights and interests (outlined above) and was manifest through three channels: changes in income levels and in income distribution, retrenchment, and curbs on workers' right to strike and participate in policy (Jonah, 1989: 140–152). Before we provide more detail to show the overall negative impact of IMF conditionality to labor in these three areas we must emphasize that the weight of IMF conditionality differed among labor groups. The impact of currency devaluation and retrenchment, for example, varied among labor, the outcome depending mainly on the sector market. To explain, we need to distinguish between tradable and non-tradable goods and services. Non-tradables are those goods and services whose prices are determined by domestic supply and demand. This is a result of the type of good involved (such as public services, housing and construction) or because the good is insulated from world markets due to transportation costs that prohibit either the import or exports of the good in question. Tradable goods are goods that cross boundaries and are theoretically determined by world market conditions. Production of cash crops for export falls in this category. (World Bank, 1990: 26–27).

Let us now use currency devaluation (a key component of IMF conditionality) to illustrate the differentiated impact of IMF conditionality on income amongst labor. Currency devaluation affects labor in three ways: as producers of tradables and non-tradables; as wage earners; and as consumers of tradables and non-tradables. Since the logic of devaluation is to cause the country's export prices to fall in dollar terms as its import prices in cedi terms rise (i.e. export more and import less) there is every reason to expect exporters as a group–in manufacturing, farming, mining, forestry, etc.—to be the immediate beneficiaries, in income terms of devaluation, while those engaged in the production of locally consumed non-tradables are to lose. In Ghana, by mid 1988, IMF conditionality had distributed income towards commercial (mainly cocoa) farmers and exporters and away from food crop farmers, low-income and landless rural workers, and the urban poor. For example, the price paid to cocoa producers increased seven-fold between 1982 and 1987, from 12,000 to 85,000 cedis per ton (West Africa, January 12, 1987: 61; Commander et al, 1989: 12). Second, as wage earners, the most likely labor groups to experience a real-wage cut following devaluation are those on fixed incomes in the formal sector (World Bank, 1990). Finally, devaluation impacts labor as consumers. By raising the official price of food, devaluation impacts labor differently depending on difference in employment and expenditure patterns. As Bentsi-Enchill noted, IMF conditionalities in Ghana, such as currency devaluation and the reduction in government spending and subsidies hit the urban population the hardest as the price of basic goods increased suddenly: water fees rose 150%; postal tariffs increased 365%; and electricity rates rose 1,000%.[46] Similarly, fuel prices increased markedly, further making the living conditions of labor deplorable. For example, the gallon price of petrol was increased from 235 cedis in 1988 to 275 in 1989, then to 360 in 1990 and then to 1,000 in 1991. Contrast with minimum daily wage, which stood at 146 cedis in 1987 and increased over time to 218 cedis in 1990.[47]

Labor was also opposed to retrenchment of workers, another key IMF conditionality.[48] Retrenchment occurred in the state enterprises, the civil service, and the local government. A survey conducted by the government's Manpower Utilization Committee, estimated that there were over 300,000 people employed in the public services, 20% of whom were underemployed. This translated into the elimination of over 45,000 positions.[49] By the end of 1990, over 45,000 civil service employees were laid off, plus 20,000 from state-owned enterprises.[50] Within the private sector, import liberalization, removal of protective tariffs, and the credit squeeze resulted in the loss of hundreds of jobs.[51]

A U.S. Congressional Mission to Ghana offered this scathing critique of the impact of retrenchment on labor.

> A significant visible group largely urban Ghanaians was clearly and dramatically disadvantaged by structural adjustment policies. These included approximately 41,000 to 45,000 'redeployed,' that is, fired civil servants (29,000 were dismissed in 1987–88 and the remainder were slated to go in 1989). 20,000 redeployed Cocoa Board employees, 20,000 state enterprise employees threatened with retrenchment over the next two years and at least hundreds of private sector employees who lost textile and other Jobs as a result of import liberation. It is worth noting that the World Bank (1984) indicated that Ghana has competitive advantage in textile production. A total of approximately 100,000 jobs have been lost.[52]

As with the devaluation, retrenchment impacted labor generally but some sector markets were disproportionately affected. The GPRTU, The Ghana Mine Workers' Union, and The Railway Workers' Union, three powerful unions within the TUC (whose workers were based in the tradable sector) gained from the adjustment policies. Mine workers, for example were given salary increases to boost productivity, while others such as the Agricultural Workers Union lost (the adjustment's redeployment exercise, for example, led to the retrenchment of 50,000 workers in the Cocoa Marketing Board alone)[53] (Hutchful, 2002: 174).

Notwithstanding the differentiated impact of IMF conditionality on labor, the TUC leadership did not relent in attacking it. Below are a couple of examples.

A resolution adopted by the TUC executive board in 1984 noted that:

> as a result of these IMF and World Bank conditions, the working people of Ghana now face unbearable conditions of life expressed in poor nutrition, high prices of goods and services, inadequate housing, continuing deterioration of social services and growing unemployment above all. . . . We caution government that the above conditions pose serious implications for the sharpening of class conflict in the society."[54]

Similarly, a statement from the TUC of 1988 noted:

> the going is still hard for the working people. . . . the sum effect of the IMF (and World Bank) sponsored economic policies are the cheapening of the local currency through the foreign exchange auction system, the high rates of unemployment and a rising cost of living brought about by the decontrolling of prices, removal and subsidies on essential goods and services and the partial freeze on wages and salaries of the working people." (TUC, 1988: 3)

A third way IMF conditionality impacted labor interests was the lack of genuine consultation and the top-down compliance with IMF conditionality by the PNDC. As noted earlier, labor as represented by the TUC felt it was an important stakeholder in Ghana's political economy and thus expected to be consulted on crucial economic issues. On numerous occasions the TUC lodged its concern of non-exclusion from national dialogue.

> The TUC has been compelled in the recent past to come out to oppose certain decisions by the authorities because it has no official communication channel to discuss issues. The authorities have failed to recognize that the TUC is a legal institution in this country (TUC Press Release, 23/4/86).

The TUC also voiced its opposition around constitutionalism. One of its press releases read:

> We recognize that our economic situation is very grave and that therefore the way to national reconstruction will impose immense tasks and sacrifices on our people. For this reason, it is imperative that options for

> national direction and development be democratically and popularly determined. Consequently, we call for the establishment of a popularly and democratically elected People's Assembly at the district, regional and national levels. The assemblies shall provide the framework for the discussion of all national issues including the promulgation of laws, and the defense and guarantee of democratic and civil liberties. We note that the absence of such a structure for the democratic exercise of the authority of the people provides for arbitrariness and violations of trade union and other democratic rights while on the other hand it contributes to the growing alienation of the people (TUC/SG/A.41/54, 20th April 1986).

Despite the fact that it generally opposed compliance with the IMF, labor was not a potent opposition force as it had historically been. Richard Jeffries finds that "Ghana [had] not experienced significant popular unrest ignited by organized or unorganized labor (or anyone else for that matter) since the massive Structural Adjustment Program was first announced in 1983." He went on to say that "labor unrest [was] nowhere as high as it was in the 1970s; indeed, strikes are currently about as low as they have ever been in Ghana. Both government and union leaders are agreed that despite the government's economic policies there has not been a significant number of protests" (Jeffries, 1991: 178).

Why was labor acquiescent? We argue that repression and co-optation are the most important factors that explain why labor unrest did not occur on any significant scale during the period under study.

The disparity in impact of the adjustment on the unions weakened or neutralized the ability of labor to channel a common platform and coherent opposition to IMF conditionalities. In July 1987, for instance, a strike action called by the TUC to protest IMF conditionalities was denounced by the Railway and Harbor Workers Union (Hutchful, 2002: 174) The differentiated impact of IMF conditionalities also made labor vulnerable to co-optation by the PNDC. Gyimah-Boadi noted that by the end of 1982, the Ghana Private Road Transport Union (GPRTU), a private and autonomous association had moved voluntarily to become embedded within the PNDC. According to him this "paid significant dividends" for both its leadership and membership, and immensely strengthened the association organizationally (Gyimah-Boadi, 1994: 132–35). The benefit that accrued to the GPRTU came in the form of lower vehicle import taxes and generally improvements in roads (meant to service the export sector) (Hutchful, 2002: 174).

To enforce compliance with IMF conditionality, the PNDC and its paramilitary supporters, also used repression (terror tactics of intimidation, coercion, and brute force) on the union leadership and supporters of the workers' cause. Exactly a week after announcing the 1983 IMF budget, the government determined to break any coalition support around labor issues equated serious opposition to IMF conditionality with subversion. The PNDC Finance Secretary Botchwey, for example, said that that "the sudden alliance between certain negative elements in society and workers following the release of the 1983 budget is an attempt by such elements to hide behind legitimate workers grievances and subvert an economic programme meant to put the economy right." (Daily Graphic, April 27, 1983).

The PNDC constantly harassed and demonized the TUC on the state-controlled media. Other times, the union leadership was arrested (Ninsin, 1991: 55). In May 1987 for example, Mr. Akwasi Adu-Amankwah, the head of the political department of the TUC, was arrested and detained on sedition charges (Hutchful, 2002:176). On June 4, 1987, workers belonging to the June Fourth movement and other PNDC supporters held a rally in front of the TUC headquarters, and later occupied the hall, refusing to move; inviting a direct confrontation with the TUC leadership.[55]

On the few occasions when workers (independently or in collaboration with others) found the courage to openly challenge the PNDC on the adjustment conditionalities through wildcat strikes and demonstrations, the government responded by dismissing the striking workers or used physical force to crush the demonstrators. In August 1987, for instance, thirty three workers of the State Gold Mining Corporation at Dunkwa mines (including the chairman, vice chairman and some executive members of the local branch of the mineworkers' union) sacked for their role in a "illegal and unofficial strike."[56] The now famous 'Kume preko' (meaning 'you may as well kill me now') demonstrations, though were successful, (in that Rawlings' government withdrew the tax),[57] is a tragic but typical example of how the PNDC treated labor demonstrations. In this particular instance, armed police and military personnel (backed by armored cars) blocked several routes in efforts to control the demonstration and protestors were routinely beaten, resulting in four deaths.

2. Students

Analysts of student movements in Africa come to the same conclusion: that no matter how radical or antiestablishment the African student sounds, they are, paradoxically, unwilling to sacrifice their privileges. Indeed, they feel like the natural heirs to the establishment. David Hapgood (1965), noted that the radicalism of African students is usually a farce. He said: "The proclaimed Marxist Leninist [of the African student] is, in his behavior, supremely bourgeois. His real interests are not the reading of Marx and Lenin but the acquiring" of material things and the maintenance of the privileges they have come to know (Hapgood, 1965; 197). The Ghanaian student movement typifies this experience. Ghanaian students, particularly the university students, have been beneficiaries of the policy-making in Ghana both in terms of the structure of the educational budget (Table 3.4) and employment (Table 3.5).

Table 3.4. Per Capita Expenditure in the Ghanaian School System 1970–1983 (constant 1983 dollars)

	1970	1975	1980
Primary	66	41	21
As % of per capita GDP	13	10	6
Secondary	100	131	66
As % of per capita GDP	20	31	17
Tertiary	-	3638	1195
As % of per capita GDP	-	900	300

Source: World Bank 1988

Table 3.5. Economically Active Population by Employment Status and Education

	Employment Status a (in percentages)				
Education Level[b]	Unemployed	Employed Private	Employed Public	Self-employed	N
None	0.6	4.3	2.6	92.4	3,024
Primary	0.8[a]	8.8	3.4	87.0	625
Secondary	3.0	13.6	18.7	64.7	2,078
University	0.0	17.9[c]	60.7	21.4[c]	28
All	1.5	8.2	8.8	81.5	5,755

Source: Ghana Living Standards Survey, *First Year Report,* April 1989, Table 55.

Notes: a. Employment status is for main or primary occupation.

b. Education Level refers to "at least some," not necessarily completed.

c. Cell contains fewer than 10 observations.

Students thus consider themselves heirs to the national elite and the trappings of power that come with it. Perhaps not intended to convey the same meaning, the National Union of Ghanaian Students (NUGS, the umbrella student organization in Ghana, which represented over 8,000 students at the country's three universities) asserted that Ghanaian "students of today are by right the inheritors of the legacies that are being put in place today."[58]

Ghanaian students are motivated by a multiplicity of interests that reinforce the prevailing view of education as privileged asset. The students' interests include effective and improved quality of education; adequate state funding and financing; guarantees of career and professional development; and autonomy from the state. An NUGS memo summarized these interests as struggles for: "the right to adequate state budgets for education; the right to an equal standard of education in all public institutions of the same level; the right to education under occupation, the right to equal access for female students to education and access specifically to traditionally male dominated fields" (Hi-Ed News, The NUGS viewpoint, March 1992: 4).

STUDENTS, IMF CONDITIONALITY AND DOMESTIC POLITICS

Like labor, the NUGS strongly supported the PNDC in the early days of the regime,[59] but became the focus for some of the most outspoken opposition as the PNDC adopted the IMF conditionalities.

The student body felt that the PNDC had betrayed them by accepting the IMF conditionalities.[60] According to Jeong, the students detested conditionalities, in particular, because it entailed cuts in education subsidies which they feared would lead to an educational system of the rich; "since the government withdrawal of these subsidies would bring extreme hardship to most students whose parents were unable to pay for college education (1995: 86–95). The NUGS noted that "the Government has already committed the country to international creditors on all the debatable issues." It then called on the PNDC to terminate the "revolution," and to transfer power to a civilian government. NUGS said it had "seen the betrayal of the principles of December 31 . . . the national economy is in a stagnated state . . . In this state of hopelessness, we the students of Ghana have no choice but to . . . call on the PNDC to hand over the reins of government to the office of the Chief Justice within a month." (quoted in Yeebo, 1985: 111).

As noted above, students were particularly unhappy about the financial aspects of the IMF conditionalities, such as de-boarding; income generation by the universities; withdrawal of government subsidies on school fees, books, and allowances; a proposed two-year national service requirement;

and the introduction of a student loan scheme (Ofuatey Kodjoe, 1998; Hutchful, 2002: 136). At its 23rd annual congress in August 1987, the NUGS addressed the impact of the IMF conditionalities on student life by announcing that "the various aspects of the planned changes in the education system would force students in boarding schools to pay higher fees as well as other charges; and these additional charges in some cases make the boarding fee three times the minimum civil service wages."[61] In a protest letter, to West Africa Magazine, the NUGS referred to the IMF conditionality as "poison," and said it "would continue to struggle till all the remnants of the obnoxious anti-worker and anti-student policies imposed by the IMF and World Bank puppets have been dismantled."[62]

The NUGS argued that education was a fundamental right of the citizen and an unshirkable responsibility of the government. It said: "We recognize the high cost of education, but stress that that in itself must not be any excuse why it should be shifted [by the government] onto the already over burdened citizens," Rather than accept the IMF conditionalities on education, the NUGS urged the PNDC to adopt a series of proposals that it (NUGS) had adopted:

1. Establishing an educational fund into which prospective donors could donate.
2. Reducing waste, duplication, etc. in the educational institutions.
3. The institutions engaging in commercial ventures to raise funds to supplement government's efforts.
4. Levying an educational tax on specific goods and services, etc.[63]

As the NUGS explained, its proposals were meant "to cushion the government, and not intended to shield the government from responsibility."

After the announcement of IMF conditionalities in April 1983, the NUGS organized a series of demonstrations on the university campuses in protest. The protests became progressively increasingly violent. On May 6, 1983 after students attacked the offices of the Ghana News Agency and two daily papers, the Government responded by announcing the indefinite closure of both the University of Ghana at Legon and the University of Kumasi on May 16. The University of Cape Coast, Ghana's third university, was closed after further violent demonstrations on July 3, 1983.[64]

Again, on May 8, 1987, the PNDC ordered the immediate closure of the nation's three universities—University of Ghana, Legon, University of Cape Coast and the University of Science and Technology at Kumasi—following demonstrations that began in March against the donor-inspired education sector.[65]

The PNDC de-emphasized the political significance of student protests and focused on the need for equity in the return on state investments, accusing the student body of being elitist. In a statement issued during the university closures, the PNDC said:

> the government will not tolerate the adventures of infantile leftists who, under the hypocritical guise of championing seemingly legitimate causes, in actual fact are seeking to create the conditions for the paralysis and destruction of certain vital national structures and institutions. The permanent closure of the university is only one of their callous designs on the insane and simplistic premise that universities are the breeding grounds for elitism, reactionaries and the bourgeoisie."[66]

The university closures not only neutralized the student protests but also created fear in the student population, whose leaders were subjected to constant harassment and surveillance by the PNDC. Kakraba Cromwell, a NUGS leader in the University of Ghana was arrested in December 1983 by the government security agencies for his alleged involvement in drug trafficking. In May 1987 (soon after the university closures), the government directed the dismissal of some of the NUGS leadership (including, Kwame Achamu, Kofi Offoe Yeboah, Kofi Gyamfi, Baidoo Ansah, Abeku Brew, Amoah Larbi, Kweku Pentsil and Arthur Kennedy). Those singles out as 'trouble makers' (such as Akoto-Ampaw, Arthur Kennedy, Baidoo Ansah, Amoah Larbi and Augustina Adjeiwah) were asked to report to the officer in charge of the Nima (a suburb in Accra) police station. The above-mentioned persons were also banned from entering any educational institution in the country, until further notice.[67]

The NUGS admitted that it had not been easy to carry across its views due to the repressive nature of the regime. The NUGS said: "we now exist under a rule of terror, an era where any view opposed to the government is crushed with weapons of destruction, where even public opinion is suppressed, press freedom is biased and the rule of law and natural justice is denied to Ghanaians."[68]

3. Army

Like most armies, distinctions exist between officers and enlisted men in the Ghanaian army.[69] Rawlings in an interview alluded to the gap between the officers and enlisted men when he said that on one occasion he had to steal "rich food" meant for senior officers for his colleagues because at that time they needed to eat well for upcoming military games. He said: "I lived for my men; that's why when I was to be shot, my men decided to sacrifice their lives for me."[70] There are however a core set of interests that are universal to the men and women in uniform.

First, the army seeks to maintain its privileged status in the society by expecting the government to consistently allocate a higher proportion of GDP to the military. And this has been the case for Ghana in the past. Though military expenditures are difficult to specify because under-reporting is common, particularly in military regimes, the data in Table 3.1 does provide a useful indication of overall magnitudes, and accurately depicts the disproportionately high ratio of Ghana's military expenditure to other essential government expenditures. Table 3.1 for example shows that, the military allocations between 1976 and 1989, were on average three times the amount allocated to transportation, energy, and communications services combined.

Second, although it recognizes and submits to the authority of civilian politicians, the Ghanaian army has always longed for, and sought to protect its institutional autonomy and has demonstrated a willingness to play a greater role in the national political arena. That Ghana had experienced five successful coup d'etats by 1982 is a testament to this fact. Indeed, Rawlings stated that "dismissals from the armed forces, divide-and-rule tactics, sometimes to the point of getting soldiers to shoot themselves" by the Limann government were part of the reasons for his second coup in December 31, 1981.[71] Laguerre's analysis of the military in Haiti is analogous to that of Ghana. According to Laguerre: "The civilian government thinks that it is its constitutional duty to [control the military]. The army thinks that it is its military duty to maintain the autonomy of the [military] institution because if the civilian government collapses, the military would remain the ultimate government to save the nation from chaos" (1993: 190–191). Like the Haitian army then, the Ghanaian army perceives itself as an "enclave government in reserve" (Laguerre, 1993: 191).

THE ARMY, IMF CONDITIONALITY AND DOMESTIC POLITICS

Recent research shows that countries with excessive military spending (in the sense that the marginal improvement in national security associated with this expenditure is less than its economic cost) also have large budget deficits and a decrease in public investment (Gupta, Schiff, and Clements, 1996). The IMF policy advice to its member countries on such spending, therefore, calls for reviewing military expenditures to identify potential fiscal savings. But because the issue of military outlay is sensitive, as it involves national security, the Fund, as a rule, does not include military expenditure in its conditionalities. As Ross Leckow, Assistant General Counsel of the IMF, noted: "while the amount which the authorities of a member spend on the military may be very important for the country's macroeconomic position, the Fund has taken the position that the question of military spending is so inherently political in nature that it could not be appropriately made the subject of conditionality."[72]

Though Rawlings came to the power with the insurgency and support of enlisted men, he abandoned this base and turned to the officer corps for support to stay in power and to enforce the IMF conditionalities. The embrace of army officers by Rawlings was a pragmatic and strategic choice.

First, Rawlings' rupture with the Left and the subsequent attempts by factions within the Left to overthrow his regime left him no option but to turn the established military structure for stability and support. Indeed, in 1982, the frequency of coup attempts made most Ghanaians write off the PNDC regime. According to Yeebo, "the PNDC had no support whatsoever from the soldiers at all. The regime was weak, unpopular, and incapable of responding to a serious rebellion . . . Military intelligence and special branch reports in 1982 indicated serious dissatisfaction in every region of the country."[73]

Rawlings was seen by most officers as a "trouble maker," who could upset their balance of privileges, in favor of the army rank. Of course, it did not help that he had executed eight senior military officers, including three former heads of state, during his first coup. To convince the officers that he considered their support vital to his regime, Rawlings, beginning in March 1983, started to distance itself from the ranks. He announced "reforms" of The Armed Forces Defence Committee (AFDCR), (composed primarily of the militant wing of enlisted men and the military Left) that the earlier PNDC leadership had created to supervise the "revolution" and to act as a separate and autonomous military institution. He restored the unified command structure that had been a staple of the army prior to the coup and restructured the AFCDRs to reflect whole units rather than just the ranks in particular units. (Hutchful, 2002: 49). That same month, he disbanded the enlisted men unit, the Boys Company, which had brought him to power.

Rawlings also moved to co-opt the military hierarchy by offering appointments. Jon Kraus notes that Rawlings turned to the officers, by offering them cabinet posts, state corporate leadership, and regional and diplomatic assignments, not because he trusted them but because he needed the officer corps to "contain coup threats and reestablish order." (Rothchild, 1991: 149).

To maintain the support of the officer corps Rawlings, or his top aides, frequently took pains to explain any new IMF conditionalities to the military, particularly the top brass (Martin, 1991: 241; Hutchful, 2002: 48).

Rawlings further supported the institutional interest of the military by increasing the wage and army benefits and upgrading the equipment of the military between 1983–1986, (Martin, 1991: 242).

Rawlings also encouraged the formation of military-civilian coalitions as a countervailing base to his tenuous support of the military, and also to reinforce the PNDC's technique of intimation on the Ghanaian populace. Thus, quasi-military security organizations that were sympathetic to Rawlings, such as the Forces Reserve Battalion, the Civil Defense Organization (CDO), Peoples Militia, the Civil Defense Organization, and Commandos all flourished and received extensive press coverage on their activities, during the revolutionary phase of Rawlings' rule. Furthermore, 'outlaw' and 'vigilante' police and military figures such as Warrant Officers Salifu Amankwa, Nkwantabisa, and Jack (who had loyal troops at their disposal) gained prominence during this era. Needless to say, these new organs and 'enforcers' terrorized civilians. According to Hutchful, these organs also engaged in "the manipulation of ethnic divisions within the military, the increased reliance on Ewe officers and troops, and the rapid rotation of key commands and postings." (Hutchful, 1997: 257–258).

4. The business entrepreneur

Our discussion on the Ghanaian business entrepreneurial class focuses on organized private capital, in particular business associations (BAs). BAs arise out of the need for a business to improve profitability and/or to improve the industry and general economic climate (Rose, 1954). In Ghana, the most influential and largest BAs are The Association of Ghana Industries (AGI) and the Ghana Chamber of Commerce (GCC) (Masten and Brown, 1995: 92).

Like businesses everywhere, Ghanaian business is motivated by one supreme interest: the pursuit of profit. There are, however, issues related to the country's legal and regulatory framework, finance, taxation and investment incentives that can prevent business from realizing this overriding objective. For the Ghanaian business to thrive there ought to be, inter alia, a climate of:

1. Improved financial intermediation, especially for credit lending.
2. Non politicization of the business climate and the demonstrated positive stance of the government toward the private sector.
3. Regular communication between the business community and the senior decision-makers of the Government.
4. Rationalization of taxation of company income and investment, and of fiscal incentives for investment.
5. The streamlining, and abolition, where appropriate, of controls, and the consistent and transparent application of policies as it

relates to the repatriation of profits and capital. (Confidential Report, Ghana: Moving Towards Sustainable Private Sector Led Growth, July 6, 1990).

BUSINESS, IMF CONDITIONALITY, AND DOMESTIC POLITICS

IMF conditionalities, such as exchange rate policies, trade liberalization, rationalization of state-run enterprises, control of inflation, and expansion of the private sector, are aimed at developing a private market-based economy. All things being equal then, IMF conditionality generally ought to empower the private sector. Paradoxically, as the PNDC complied with IMF conditionalities, it was at the same time hostile and mistrustful of private business. For example, while it enacted numerous legislation to increase private capital participation in the Ghanaian economy (e.g. The Investment Code, 1985 (P.N.D.C.L. 116),[74] Investment Code (Amendment) Law, 1992 (P.N.D.C.L. 292); Investment Code (Area of Special Priority) Instrument, 1991 (L.I. 1519); and Investment Code (Immigrant Quota) Regulations, 1992 (L.I. 1543), the PNDC continued to antagonize private (especially indigenous) capital and did not maintain a proactive complementary relationship with it. Not surprisingly, the business community in turn remained ambivalent in attitude to the PNDC regime.

First, the anti-capitalist rhetoric and political actions during the heyday of the 'revolution' still weighed on the minds of business. During this period, apart from the freeze in the bank accounts of individuals and businesses with bank deposits in excess of 50,000 cedis, countless number of manufacturing firms (such as Mr. J. K. Siaw, owner of the Tata Brewery Company; Dr. Sarfo Adu who set up the Industrial Chemical Company (ICL) to manufacture drugs for both the domestic and export market; Mr. Appiah Menka who manufactured Apino soap and other products; Dr. Ato Addison of Cement Works; Mr. Appenteng Mensah of Panbros Salt; and Mr. B.A. Mensah of International Tobacco) were confiscated (Adjei, 1984).

Commenting on the PNDC's anti-business crusade and the subsequent alienation of much of the private business community before the ERP, Jon Kraus recalled that: "businessmen, among others, were subject during the revolutionary years of 1982–83 to intensive interrogation, searches, precipitate arrest and denial of the rule of law" (2002: 401). But the antagonistic and punitive directives against the private sector did not end with the adoption of IMF reform. Indeed, they continued (Kraus, 2002: 404–405). Oelbaum (2002: 307) cites instances where Rawlings used extralegal measures to undermine the interests of entrepreneurs he considered 'oppositional.' For example, the factory of Kwame Safo Adu, a medical doctor was confiscated in 1989 by the PNDC on charges of economic sabotage, and yet was not returned when Safo Adu was found not guilty of the charges in 1991 (Kraus, 2002: 404).

In the eyes of the PNDC (especially to Rawlings), private capital had an inherent potential for exploitation and abuse, and thus needed close monitoring. Rawlings' thinking is apparent in a 'welcome' speech to potential foreign investors, hosted by the Ghana Investment Center (GIC) and the World Bank's Multilateral Investment Center Agency (MIGA) in February 1990. After recounting the exploitative nature of colonialism in Ghana, and outlining examples of corrupt multinational investment activity, Rawlings stated: "I can assure you that you are very truly welcome . . . But I am obliged to emphasize that we cannot however tolerate foreign investors who think that because Ghana is a small developing country, they can arrogantly throw their weight around."[75]

Apart from its antagonistic posture to business, the PNDC also purposely excluded BAs from any discussions on economic policy (Kraus, 2002: 405). The business communities were not players in the launching of the reforms and were, for the most part, marginalized in the management of its compliance (World Bank, 1990: 50). This sense of marginalization contributed to the business community's guarded response to the adjustment program (Bentsi-Enchill, 1988: 17).

The business community also felt that the PNDC was more interested in acquiring international, rather than domestic capital. Tangri (1992: 102) made this poignant observation in his survey of Ghanaian business. He said "the regime was not perceived as sufficiently supportive of the economic interests of domestic capital . . . indeed it was viewed as destroying Ghanaian capital by not assisting local concerns to stand up to the rigors of international competition." The president of the GCC similarly alluded to this when, in a speech, in 1991 he said foreign investment would only be attracted when local investors were seen to be looked upon favorably by their own government. As a consequence of the PNDC's actions, BAs though welcoming of IMF conditionality, remained adamant about throwing its full support behind the program. (Oelbaum, 2002: 307).

Be that as it may, the initial impact of IMF conditionality to private capital varied by sector and size. For example, large-scale domestic enterprises (LSE) experienced a substantial negative impact compared to small-scale enterprise (SSE). Numerous analysts have made this point. Nikoi (1996), for example, has argued, that with liberalization and the free convertibility of the exchange rate, multinational corporations (MNCs), rather than local capital, are in a unique position to take advantage of economies of scale, of low labor and imported input costs, and of global market information. Killick (1989) states that the major gainers of adjustment measures, such as devaluation, were usually large local and foreign capitalists who invested in export-oriented sectors, including gold mining, timber industry, and other capital-intensive raw material producing industries. Harvey (1991: 25) similarly notes that adjustment benefited import and export merchants, and generated hefty salaries for business executives who had access to foreign capital. Lastly, Steel and Webster (1993) also showed that abolishing restrictive licensing, tax incentives and credit allocations, that had been characteristic of Ghana's industrial structure negatively impacts LSEs, whilst presenting previously untapped opportunities for SSEs.

Table 3.6 shows the average annual growth in employment by firm size during 1975–83 and 1983–89 for sample firms established by 1975. As the table reveals, during 1975–83, incomes fell and import controls were tightened as foreign exchange became increasingly scarce. Nevertheless, employment grew at 7.6% a year in the medium- and large-scale firms in the sample, presumably because imports were channeled to these firms. The situation however reversed under IMF conditionalities from 1983 to 1989, with employment falling sharply in the medium to large sample firms due to greater competition from liberalized imports and increasing costs of imported inputs (due to the effect of devaluation).

Table 3.6. Employment Growth, by Age and Size of Firm, 1975–83 and 1983–89 (weighted average annual percentage growth)

	Growth since start						
	Firms established By 1975		*Established by*	*Established During*	*Number of firms established by*		
Firm size	*1975–83*	*1983–89*	*1983*	*1984–89*	*1975*	*1983*	*1989*
1–3 workers	0.0	16.0	9.7	7.6	4	17	33
4–9 workers	-0.2	6.2	1.3	45.1	7	16	26
10–29 workers	0.5	3.1	8.1	19.1	9	9	16
30 + workers	7.6	-17.2	1.1	n.a.	5	7	7

n.a. Not applicable.

Note: Size categories and weights are based on total employment in 1983 for firms established by then, to reveal the impact according to firm size at the beginning of adjustment. For firms established from 1984 to 1988, size categories are based on 1989 employment and weights on employment at start-up.

Source: Steel and Webster, 1993: 429

CONCLUSION

The politics of compliance with IMF adjustment in Ghana gives credence to several assumptions in the academic literature on the politics of reform. First, Ghana's case shows that the ability to enforce compliance with IMF conditionality lay in the PNDC's ability to reshape the domestic political structures in order to contain political cost and reduce risks. (Risk, as used here, refers to the difficulties of predicting and hence controlling the costs of adjustment). As Atta Mills (1989: 21–23) has observed "the social and political costs of compliance with conditionalities are not evenly distributed in the society. While in the long term the costs (and benefits) might be distributed more evenly, in the short term, managing the uneven distribution of costs requires a careful assessment of the gains and losses, the winners and losers, and the mobilization of the winners in support of the program."[76] The PNDC realizing that the preexisting domestic social structure provided the most secure support base (*ala* the national elite) shifted its allegiance away from students, labor and radicals, who apart from lacking political power lacked an alternative vision to IMF conditionality.

The literature on the politics of reform also posits that implementing and sustaining neoliberal adjustment policies is politically problematic because of asymmetries in costs and benefits. Haggard and Kaufman (1992: 18) explain that "the central political dilemma is that though significant benefits may accrue to society as a whole, policy adjustment involves significant startup costs and the reduction of rents to particular groups." Because of this perceived tension between economic and political rationality, Joan Nelson (1990: 325) writes that "adjustment measures by their nature arouse considerable opposition and win few immediate friends." To enforce compliance, many political scientists have concluded that only strong and relatively autonomous governments (one relatively insulated from political pressures and social interests) can carry reforms through. In the words of Nelson: "concentrated authority directly facilitates implementation; it also heightens the credibility of programs, crucially shaping both political and economic responses" (Nelson, 1990: 25). As we have seen, the case of Ghana under the PNDC typifies this leadership profile: the Rawlings regime was able to initiate reform primarily because the Ghanaian population was intimidated and exhausted with fear. According to Yeebo "the PNDC was the most brutal regime in Ghanaian history. . . . The brutality of the period is still underestimated by many mainly because of ignorance."[77] And, as Markovitz reminds us, a political regime that is willing to invest the necessary time and resources to "institutionalize and organize the process of terror on a steady and rational basis. . . . . . . may overcome resistance and secure cooperation (Markovitz, 1977: 322). Dr. Adu Boahen's now famous quote shows the extent to which terror had taken hold of the populace and captures the sentiment prevalent at the initiation of adjustment. He said: "We have not protested or staged riots not because we trust the PNDC but because we fear the PNDC! We are afraid of being detained, liquidated or dragged before the CVC or NIC or being subjected to all sorts of molestation" (Boahen, 1989: 51).

Chapter Four

Compliance with IMF Conditionality and the Politics of Power: 1983–2000

> "This government has no intention of subordinating the nation's economic interests to political expedience."
>
> —Ghana's President, Jerry John Rawlings (1996)

INTRODUCTION

The previous chapter detailed the key socio-economic groups affected by IMF conditionality, and the strategies employed by the PNDC to enforce compliance. This chapter shifts the focus of inquiry to the issue of PNDC's compliance record with a view to identifying the periods of non-compliance and the factors that contributed to the suspension or violation of the terms of IMF conditionalities.

The chapter is divided into three sections. Section one recounts the years 1983 to 2000, describing each IMF loan or facility and the terms of the related conditionality which the PNDC entered into with the IMF. Section two provides a general overview of the compliance record of the PNDC, identifying periods of non-compliance (using the methodology describe in Chapter 1), and describing what was happening within Ghana during each period of non-compliance. Section three, the concluding section, specifies and analyzes the links and connections, if any, between non-compliance (our dependent variable) and political factors (our independent variables).

To provide a context to the arrangements and conditionalities that the PNDC entered with the IMF, this section provides first a summary of all the

IMF loan or facilities that the PNDC negotiated with the IMF; and second an overview of the major components and objectives of the conditionalities agreed to.

SUMMARY OF IMF LOAN OR FACILITY WITH GHANA: 1983–2000

The government of Jerry Rawlings agreed to eight IMF programs between August 1983 and November 2000 (see Table 4.1 for exact date and type of loan).[1]

The first was a Compensatory Financing Facility (CFF) loan in 1983. The CFF was established in 1963 to provide resources to IMF member countries, particularly exporters of primary products, to cover shortfalls in export earnings and services receipts, as well as excesses in cereal import costs, that are temporary and arise from events beyond the members' control.[2]

The second type of loan negotiated by the PNDC was two Standby loans in 1984 and 1986. Although there is no mention of it in the IMFs Articles of Agreement (or in subsequent amendments), by 1969, the stand-by arrangement/loan, had developed as the main instrument through which the IMF disbursed short-term loans (not more than three years) to member countries, as long as the member observed the performance criteria and other terms specified in the arrangement.[3]

A simultaneous Extended Fund Facility (EFF) arrangement and Structural Adjustment Facility (SAF) loan was concluded in 1987. The EFF is similar to the Standby Loan and was created in 1974 to offer medium-term assistance to IMF members. In the decision establishing the EFF, the IMF Executive Board stressed that it must focus on persistent structural balance of payments maladjustments.[4] In 1986, the IMF for the first time explicitly created a financing facility, the SAF, to support structural reform by providing balance-of-payments assistance to low-income countries on concessional terms. Its objective was to help the member country move toward restoring a viable balance-of-payments position and sustainable growth.

The PNDC also contracted two Enhanced SAF (ESAF) loans in 1988 and 1995 respectively. The IMF in 1987 established the Enhanced Structural Adjustment Facility (ESAF) to replace the SAF. The ESAF arrangements are made available to eligible countries undertaking three-year comprehensive macroeconomic and structural adjustment programs. Central to the arrangements are Policy Framework Papers (PFPs), which are forward-looking documents drafted by the national authorities in collaboration with the staffs of the IMF and the World Bank.

Table 4.1. Ghana's History of Lending Arrangements with the IMF: 1983–2000 (In millions of SDRs)

Facility	Date of Arrangement	Date of Expiration or Cancellation	Amount Agreed	Amount Drawn	Amount Outstanding
PRGF2 Trust Fund	5/3/99	11/30/02	228,800	176,218	149,465
Enhanced Structural Adjustment Facility	6/30/95	5/2/99	109,600	82,200	82,200
Enhanced Structural Adjustment Facility	6/30/95	5/2/99	54,800	54,800	38,360
SAF Resources under PRGF Arrangements	11/9/88	3/5/92	102,250	102,250	0
Structural Adjustment Facility Arrangement	11/11/87	11/9/88	129,858	40,900	0
Enhanced Structural Adjustment Facility	11/9/88	3/5/92	286,300	286,300	0
Extended Arrangements	11/6/87	11/8/88	245,400	97,550	0
Stand-By Arrangements	10/15/86	10/14/87	81,800	81,800	0
Stand-By Arrangements	8/27/84	12/31/85	180,000	180,000	0
Compensatory Financing Facility	08/01/83	08/01/84	120,500	120,500	0
Total			1,539,308	1,222,518	270,025

Source: IMF Annual Reports (1983–2000)

The final loan facility negotiated by the PNDC was two Poverty Reduction and Growth Facility Arrangements (PRGF) loans in 1988 and 1999. The PRGF, which replaced the Enhanced Structural Adjustment Facility (ESAF) in November 1999, are provided to support macroeconomic and structural adjustment programs. They are made in support of three-year programs and carry an annual interest rate of 0.5%, with a 5½ year grace period and 10- year maturity. The purpose of the PRGF facility is "to support programs to strengthen substantially and in a sustainable manner [qualifying low-income members] balance of payments position and to foster durable growth, leading to higher living standards and a reduction in poverty."[5] The new name is intended to convey the message that this facility is focused on poverty reduction as well as on the structural adjustments needed to promote growth (IMF, November 22, 1999).[6]

Overall, the total amount of IMF financial resources committed to Ghana during 1983–2000 amounted to SDR 1.53 billion. In dollar value, this is a little more than $2 billion.

THE MAJOR COMPONENTS AND OBJECTIVES OF IMF CONDITIONALITIES: 1983–2000

The PNDC's Economic Recovery Programme (ERP) and associated IMF conditionalities was implemented in three phases during the period 1983 through 2000. These phases may be considered part of a continuum rather than discrete segments.

The first phase, the ERP I, launched in the April 1983 budget, was set in a three-year time frame (1983–86).

The specific objectives of the ERP I were:

1. to restore incentives for production of food, industrial raw materials and export commodities and thereby increase their output to modest but realistic levels;
2. to increase the availability of essential consumer goods and improve the distribution system;
3. to increase the overall availability of foreign exchange in the country, improve its allocation mechanism and channel it into selected high priority activities;
4. to lower the rate of inflation by pursuing prudent fiscal, monetary and trade policies;
5. to rehabilitate the physical infrastructure of the country in support of directly productive activities;
6. to undertake systematic analyses and studies leading towards a major restructuring of economic institutions in the country; and
7. to improve the tarnished image of Ghana in international financial circles through effective debt and foreign exchange reserve management, and thus restoring confidence in the economy with overseas banking and suppliers establishments.[8]

The second phase, the ERP II, launched in the 1986 budget, covered the period 1986–1991. At the core of the ERP II was a Structural Adjustment Program, which had as its key macroeconomic targets, sustained growth in GDP, reduction of inflation, and rehabilitation of physical and productive infrastructure.[9]

The specific objectives of the ERP II were:

1. to sustain economic growth at between 5 to 5.5% per annum over the medium term;
2. to increase the level of public investment from about 10% of national income to about 25% by the end of the decade;
3. to increase domestic savings from about 7% of GDP at the end of ERP I to about 15% by the end of the decade;
4. to stimulate substantial increase in the levels of savings and investment in the economy through appropriate monetary instruments, including interest rates, and steps to further improve confidence in the financial system and in the banking institutions;
5. to improve public sector management through specific initiatives. These initiatives include rationalizing State-owned enterprises through liquidations, mergers, divestitures, etc., and placing them on a firmer financial footing through better corporate planning, adequate capitalization, and improved management; and
6. to effectively mobilize the resources generated to improve the social and overall well-being of the people of Ghana, particularly the underprivileged, deprived, and the vulnerable.[10]

The third phase began in earnest in 1992, when the core objective of the IMF adjustment package began stressing and integrating poverty reduction with macroeconomic policies. The new pro-poor and pro-growth strategy came about because the IFIs began to recognize that acute poverty and severe inequality in economic opportunities and asset endowments can themselves be obstacles to growth (IMF, 1993).

The principal objectives of the third phase, poverty reduction strategy, were:

1. a reduction in the incidence of poverty in both rural and urban areas;
2. strengthened capabilities of the poor and vulnerable to earn income;
3. reduced gender and geographical disparities; and
4. a healthier, better-educated and more productive population

To achieve these poverty reduction goals, the government outlined a series of strategies that included:

1. accelerating economic growth with equity through the use of sound macro-economic policies, which emphasize employment generation;
2. gradually developing firm targets for poverty reduction and improving the database on poverty with a view to ensuring more effective poverty programming;
3. strengthening the agricultural sector by improving productivity;
4. broadening and deepening the manufacturing and services sectors;
5. increasing investment in human resources through improving the quality and access to education, health services, nutrition, water, and sanitation;
6. encouraging the development of an indigenous entrepreneurial class; and
7. reducing the isolation of poor communities through strengthening economic infrastructure, such as roads and communication networks (IMF, 1999).

The major policy conditionalities[11] deployed to achieve the goals and objectives of the reform programs, outlined above, may be grouped under three main headings:

1. Demand restraint—which involved placing ceilings on credit expansion, budget constraints, and wage restraint. As stated in Chapter 1, the objective of the IMF's conditionalities is to enable the adjusting country to eliminate its balance of payment deficit (i.e. to enable the country to pay its foreign creditors). And one way to do this, at least in the short term (and IMF loans are of short-term maturity, usually one to three years), is to restrain demand, by embarking on contractionary monetary and fiscal policies.
2. Switching of resources to "tradeables"—exports and efficient import substitutes, by means of currency depreciation and price reforms.
3. Policies aimed at the improvement of the medium and long-term efficiency of the economy, e.g., financial sector reform, import liberalization, state enterprises reform, public sector management improvement, etc. (Nyanteng, 1993).

OVERVIEW OF THE COMPLIANCE RECORD OF THE PNDC

We will now examine the PNDC's record vis-à-vis IMF conditionalities (listed above). The implementation record of Ghana's ERP programs (1983–2000) reveals that the PNDC achieved a remarkable degree of compliance with Fund conditions. As IMF's Corbo and Fisher intimated in 1995, "Ghana . . . has been the most successful of the African adjusters." (1995: 25). However, on four separate occasions, several key IMF conditionalities, relating to monetary and fiscal policies were not met. The four instances of noncompliance occurred during the following the periods: January-March 1986; August 1992-December 1992; July–November 1996; and September–November 2000.

The PNDC's noncompliance with IMF conditionalities occurred mainly in the form of excessive unbudgeted spending or large fiscal slippages, such as granting substantial wage increases and relaxing tax collection. It is important to stress that contractionary monetary and fiscal policies formed a core part of IMF conditionality due to Ghana's weak public finance. For example, Ghana's tax revenue, as a percentage of GDP, had declined from 13.8% in 1975 to 4.6% by 1983. Government expenditure, as a percentage of GDP, fell from 20% in 1980 to 10.2% in 1982, with the ratio of current-to-capital expenditure increasing from 3.8 in 1975 to 10.2 by 1982. This state of affairs moved the budget from a surplus of 2.3% of GDP in 1970–71 to a deficit of 14.7% of GDP by 1980–81 (Bawumi, 1996: 113–133). Not surprisingly, a strengthened fiscal and monetary position became a core objective of Ghana's economic adjustment programs supported by IMF lending. Thus unbudgeted expansionary fiscal and monetary policies (such as increases in cash/wealth transfers to households, employment and profit opportunities from public investment projects, reductions in tax rates, increase in net claims on government by the banking system, and the delayed collection of taxes) by the Ghanaian government was sure to lead to noncompliance since they either led to lower government revenue or increased public expenditure than programmed.

THE PERIODS OF NON-COMPLIANCE

We shall now describe what was happening within Ghana before, and during each period of non-compliance.

NONCOMPLIANCE (1): JANUARY-APRIL 1986

Government and Political Developments and Noncompliance Activity by the PNDC

After three years of successfully complying with IMF conditionality, the PNDC, in the first quarter of 1986, registered its first act of noncompliance. Concerned about the volatile political environment, the PNDC, contra to

IMF conditionality, placated labor (a key social group, as shown in Chapter 3) by granting substantial wage increases.

The PNDC faced considerable political challenges in its efforts to comply with the IMF conditionalities (see previous chapter). By 1985, the government had weathered numerous coup attempts and clamped down on the increasingly vocal protest from politically significant sectors of society. These protests were mainly centered in the urban areas and came from those sectors that were most adversely affected by conditionalities, such as civil servants and other wage and salaried workers.

In 1985–1986, however, the level of political violence/instability, expressed in the forms of coup attempts, labor strikes and dissident activity, reached its peak. The following is an illustration of the incidents and events that occurred in Ghana prior to the PNDC's first major act of noncompliance with IMF conditionality in 1986. Taken together, these incidents and events show that the tenure of the PNDC regime between January–April 1986 had become more precarious than at any other time in its political life and that becoming noncompliant with IMF conditionality by granting large wage increases, was a politically expedient action for survival.

COUPS, INSURGENTS AND DISSIDENTS

The first potential destabilizing activity during this period occurred in the form of coups, insurgents and dissidents. While there were at least about thirteen coup attempts between 1983 and 1985, there were at least seven coup attempts in the years 1985 and 1986 alone. Notable amongst these was the plot to assassinate Flt.-Lt. Rawlings on January 31, 1985 at Kumasi (Ghana's second largest city, some 270 km north of Accra). The assassination plot was foiled after the alleged conspirators decided to postpone the attempt for fear that it might lead to excessive casualties. Five members of the armed forces and one civilian (Maj. John Ocran, Sgt. Francis Yaovi Anku, Sgt. Joseph Issaka, Maj. Hamlet Akwasi-Anto and Mr. Shaibu Ibrahim and Sgt. Oduro Frimpong) were arrested on February 2 for 'plotting to destabilize the country' and subsequently found guilty and executed on May 25.[12]

Also on December 11, 1985, the state owned paper The Peoples' Daily Graphic' reported the arrest of three Ghanaian citizens in Newark, New Jersey by U.S. customs officials on charges that they had conspired to buy missiles, anti-aircraft guns and other weapons to arm the Ghanaian Democracy Movement, (an exile opposition group) for subversive activities against the PNDC. The three were named as: J.H. Mensah, a Finance Minister in the Busia regime, Joseph Boateng, a taxi driver in New York, and Kwasi Baidoo, a computer technician living in Dover, New Jersey. The paper noted that:

> "those who have posed as responsible and patriotic citizens of Ghana unjustly exiled now stand exposed as deceivers. They have joined hands with disgruntled and ambitious pseudo-revolutionaries whose only common ground is the lust for power and position, and to attain their aim, they are prepared to plunge the country into chaos" (editorial).

Another plot by dissidents to destabilize the PNDC regime was uncovered on March 18, 1986. This incident was uncovered in Brazil, when a ship carrying an illegal cargo of six tons of ammunition and military equipment was intercepted. The ship, Nobistor, with its crew of 18, made up of 10 Argentineans and eight U.S. citizens were arrested off the Brazilian coast, bound for Ghana. According to the police in Rio de Janeiro, the ship also carried maps and instructions for an operational attack on several civilian and military targets in Accra. In hearings later in Brazil, it was revealed that the ammunition and military equipment were purchased by a group of Ghanaian dissidents led by one Godfried Osei, who had tried several times to destabilize the PNDC.[13]

CIA ACTIVITIES CHARGED

The second potential destabilizing activity during this period occurred in the form heightened clandestine CIA activity in Ghana. Rawlings, in particular believed that the U.S. Central intelligence Agency (CIA) was behind the numerous attempts to overthrow his regime (see section three, below). If those fears were not fueled when eight Americans were convicted in Brazil of trying to smuggle six tons of ammunition to rebels in Ghana (see above) in June 1985, they certainly were when Ghana uncovered a CIA operation in its midst and one of the CIA's Ghanaian operatives was murdered in September 1985.

The PNDC was tipped off by the clandestine CIA when a low-level American clerk for the CIA station in Virginia passed details of the operation, including names of informants, to her Ghanaian lover, who happened to be Rawlings' cousin. The PNDC subsequently arrested eight Ghanaians in Accra on charges of spying for the CIA in September 1985. The clerk, Sharon M. Scranage, and her lover, Michael Agbotui Soussoudis, were arrested while in the United States. Scranage pleaded guilty to charges of transmitting classified information on CIA operations to Soussoudis, and he pleaded no contest to seeking such information from her. Both were sentenced to prison. But a deal was worked out between the two countries: Ghana agreed to allow the eight accused spies to leave the country, and the United States agreed to allow Rawlings' cousin, Soussoudis, to return to Ghana, although Scranage remained in prison. It was further agreed that Ghana would be allowed to announce the swap. But on November 24, the announcement was made instead by the U.S. Justice Department. Ghana promptly expelled four U.S. diplomats out of the country, and the United States responded in kind, expelling four Ghanaian diplomats. Still, the prisoner exchange went through.[14]

POPULAR ANTI-REGIME PROTESTS AND PNDC CAPITULATION

The third potential destabilizing activity during this period occurred in the form of national strikes by public and private labor unions. First, the country's financial institutions embarked on a strike in January 1986, and the Ashanti Goldfields Corporation, the largest private-sector employer and a major foreign exchange earner, went on a 10-day strike at the end of March 1986 to demand higher wages and better working conditions, respectively. But by far the most potentially serious general strike was the TUC-led action planned for April 15, 1986, which was only narrowly averted after the PNDC caved in to the demands of the opposition coalition. According to the Matthew Martin (1991: 243), the trade unions had a major effect in 1986 because "they were joined by civil servants, lower army ranks, and students." Below are details on the events that lead to the threat of a national stoppage by the TUC and the PNDC's subsequent capitulation and ultimate noncompliance with aspects of IMF conditions attached to wage policy.

On January 11, 1986, the PNDC announced a 50% devaluation of the Cedi (C), to a new rate of 1.00 U.S. dollars= 90 Cedis, which it said was designed to ensure more profitable exports and greater efficiency in domestic production. At the same time, the government announced a 28.6% increase in the minimum wage from 70 Cedis to 90 Cedis a day, together with marginal reductions in income tax, which were intended to cushion the workers from the blow of yet another devaluation (the ninth since the IMF program began).

Ten days later, January 21, 1986, thousands of workers demonstrated in Tema, an industrial center outside Accra, in protest at the devaluation of the national currency and what they considered an insufficient hike in the minimum wage. A TUC resolution said: "a 30% increase in the basic wage announced earlier this month by the government had failed to increase workers' real incomes. . . . many employers were unable to pay the new minimum wage . . . because of adverse effects on their businesses from a 50% devaluation of the currency, the cedi, enacted in tandem with the pay hike."[15]

However, in the Government's haste to relieve some of the effects of the latest devaluation by granting wage and benefit increases, it destroyed existing IMF conditionalities: The government wages and salaries bill rose 112% to C 30 billion, from C 14 billion in 1985, well above the IMF target (stipulated in the 1985 budget) of a 70% increase.

The PNDC initially blamed the large increase on an arithmetical error in calculating the new rises, but attempts to impose an arithmetical solution to erase the C 4 billion to C 5 billion excess met with staunch union opposition. After issuing, and then withdrawing, five separate sets of guidelines on the increases—causing total confusion in both the public and private sector—the Government attempted to solve the problem by abolishing one of the 100 or so non-taxable allowances which workers then enjoyed. The move was met by the threat of a national stoppage by labor. The PNDC subsequently backed down and reinstated the original allowance.[16]

The IMF reacted, in late April 1986, by suspending disbursements under the second stand-by arrangement. (And the World Bank, following the Fund, delayed by 90 days disbursements of its sector loans). The IMF was not against a minimum wage increase per se, and indeed the Fund staff mission in December 1985[17] had made such a recommendation to the PNDC. According to the IMF, the economy-wide increase of the minimum wage, which in 1985 was still only about 30% of its 1972 level in real terms, was thought justified by price and real sector developments, including increases in productivity that accompanied higher rates of capacity utilization. The additional incentives to the civil servants were thought necessary to increase efficiency of public administration. The Fund staff mission envisaged an overall increase of the civil service wage bill (excluding allowances) of some 70% relative to its 1985 base, 28.6% reflecting the increase in the minimum wage and 32% reflecting the adjustment of relativities. However, the wage and salary adjustment actually announced in January by the PNDC would have generated around 147% higher than its 1985 base, more than twice the IMF target. The IMF's position (and reason for suspending disbursements) was that developments in the areas of credit policy and wage policies during the last few months of 1985 and in the early part of 1986 had the potential of undermining the stabilization gains obtained since 1983.[18]

Under Article IV of the IMF's Articles of Agreement, the IMF holds bilateral discussions with members, usually every year. A staff team visits the country, collects economic and financial information, and discusses with officials the country's economic developments and policies.

On return to headquarters, the staff prepares a report, which forms the basis for discussion by the Executive Board. At the conclusion of the discussion, the Managing Director, as Chairman of the Board, summarizes the views of Executive Directors, and this summary is transmitted to the country's authorities.

The Ghanaian authorities met their IMF counterparts in Accra[19] between June 15 and July 2, 1986 to try and break the impasse and continue discussions on the proposed stand-by arrangement. The Ghanaian representatives included Dr. Botchwey, PNDC Secretary for Finance and Economic Planning, Dr. J. Addo, Governor of the Bank of Ghana, Dr. Abbey, Ghana's High Commissioner to Canada, and Messrs. Obeng, PNDC Coordinating Secretary, and Ahwoi, PNDC Revenue Secretary, among others. The IMF representatives were Messrs. Kratz (head-AFR), Lorie (AFR). Hemming (FAD), Thomsen (ETR), Young (EP-AFR), and Ms. Canizares (secretary-AFR). They were assisted by Mr. Sharer, the fund resident representative in Accra. Mr. Salehkhou, Executive Director representing Ghana, participated in some of the policy discussions. Both sides met again in Accra and Washington during August and early September 1986.

The PNDC/IMF impasse was finally broken due to greater flexibility on the part of the IMF (reflected in their 'concession' to the PNDC's proposal for the managed foreign exchange auction—see IMF press statement on approving the second stand-by arrangement in October 1986 below) and promises of increased external aid flows secured at the 4th Donors Conference in late 1986. The PNDC, for its part, agreed to (1) roll back part of the wage increases and announced a 25% pay cut on civil servants in June 1986 and (2) to cancel the payment of most allowances to civil servants during the last quarter of 1986, resulting in a reduction of the projected government wage bill by 4.5 billion cedis to 26.3 billion cedis.[20]

The IMF finally, on October 17, 1986, announced its approval of a 12-month standby credit arrangement of 81.8 million SDRs to Ghana. The Fund noted that:

> far-reaching adjustment measures implemented by the Ghanaian authorities since 1983, including a 92.8 percent real depreciation of the cedi, supported by the liberalization of domestic prices, have dramatically shifted incentives back to Ghana's most productive sectors and at the same time restored a substantial part of the government's tax base . . . The recently instituted foreign exchange auction system[21] besides broadening access to the foreign exchange market, was designed (together with a liberalization of the import-licensing system) to ensure that foreign exchange for the importation of raw materials and equipment would go to the most

efficient users, to enhance Ghana's competitive position, and to encourage remittances and capital inflows. (IMF Press Release No. 86/53)

NONCOMPLIANCE AND GHANA'S ELECTIONS

The second, third and fourth noncompliance with IMF conditionalities that we have identified occurred prior to, or during, election periods. We found that the PNDC, concerned about securing the support of labor unions and other important sections of the electorate, such as the rural dwellers, became noncompliant with IMF conditionalities through excessive expenditure increases directed to these groups.

Ghana has organized three (1992, 1996, 2000) presidential and parliamentary elections since the transition to multi-party democracy in 1992. We will first examine each election period, specifying the PNDC's noncompliance, and then proceed to analyze the relationship between elections and noncompliance.

NONCOMPLIANCE (2): AUGUST–DECEMBER 1992

Government and political developments and noncompliance activity by the PNDC

The year 1992 marked the third phase of the IMF supported adjustment program. The year was also a watershed in the political and constitutional history of Ghana: a new constitution reintroducing democratic rule was adopted in April, and presidential and parliamentary elections (its first elections in over a decade) followed in November and December, respectively.

The 1992 elections brought in its wake escalating political pressures for Rawlings' PNDC regime. Doctors went on strike in May, nurses in June, workers of the Cocoa Board in July, and railway employees and civil servants in September. With the presidential and parliamentary elections due in November and December, respectively, and the government bent on securing labor and rural support in particular and the general population as a whole, Rawlings' team manipulated fiscal policy, and became noncompliant with IMF conditionalities. Following are the details of the PNDC's macroeconomic profligacy.

The PNDC granted a large wage increase to the civil servants, which intended to reduce the continuing large disparities between the civil service and the rest of the public sector. The increase consisted of across-the-board salary adjustment averaging about 80% of the nominal payroll, effective as of July 1, 1992 (See Table 4.2). The large increase in civil service wages

Table 4.2. Central Government Expenditure (as percentage of GDP)

	1990	1991	1992	1993	1994	1995	1996	1997	1998	1999
(In percent of total expenditure)										
Total expenditure	100.1	100.0	100.0	100.0	100.0	100.0	100.0	100.0	100.0	100.0
Recurrent expenditure	60.4	58.9	58.1	61.7	57.3	53.9	55.2	57.1	60.5	62.8
Noninterest expenditure	52.4	49.7	49.2	49.8	43.1	39.9	38.0	35.4	36.1	41.4
Wages and salaries	24.1	22.8	24.8	20.2	18.3	18.3	18.2	18.4	19.4	21.5
Goods and services	13.2	13.1	10.0	12.6	10.5	8.1	7.2	6.9	7.5	9.2
Subsidies and transfers	15.1	13.8	14.4	17.0	14.3	13.6	12.6	10.1	9.3	10.9
Interest	8.0	9.2	8.9	12.0	14.2	13.9	17.2	21.7	24.3	21.3
Domestic	5.1	6.4	5.1	8.4	10.3	9.9	12.9	15.8	18.3	16.2
External	2.9	2.8	3.8	3.6	3.9	4.1	4.3	5.9	6.1	5.2
Capital expenditure	39.6	41.1	41.9	38.3	42.7	46.1	44.8	42.9	39.5	37.2
Domestic	16.9	17.0	19.1	12.7	14.6	22.2	20.2	13.3	15.4	15.8
Foreign-financed	22.7	24.1	22.9	25.5	28.1	23.9	24.5	29.7	24.2	21.5
(As percentage of GDP)										
Total expenditure	16.8	18.0	24.6	29.0	31.2	30.4	29.7	29.0	28.6	26.2
Recurrent expenditure	10.1	10.6	14.3	17.9	17.9	16.4	16.4	16.5	17.3	16.4
Noninterest expenditure	8.8	8.9	12.1	14.4	13.4	12.1	11.3	10.3	10.3	10.8

Wages and salaries	4.0	4.1	6.1	5.9	5.7	5.6	5.4	5.3	5.5	5.6
Goods and services	2.2	2.4	2.5	3.6	3.3	2.5	2.1	2.0	2.1	2.4
Subsidies and transfers	2.5	2.5	3.5	4.9	4.5	4.1	3.8	2.9	2.7	2.8
Interest	1.3	1.7	2.2	3.5	4.4	4.2	5.1	6.3	7.0	5.6
Domestic	0.9	1.2	1.2	2.4	3.2	3.0	3.8	4.6	5.2	4.2
External	0.5	0.5	0.9	1.0	1.2	1.2	1.3	1.7	1.7	1.4
Capital expenditure	6.7	7.4	10.3	11.1	13.3	14.0	13.3	12.4	11.3	9.8
Domestic	2.8	3.1	4.7	3.7	4.5	6.8	6.0	3.8	4.4	4.1
Foreign-financed	3.8	4.3	5.6	7.4	8.8	7.3	7.3	8.6	6.9	5.6

Source: IMF

was also reflected in the changes in the functional composition of expenditures in 1992. Labor intensive services, like education, health, general public services (including security services), economic services, and defense, all increased in real terms. In particular, the share in total central government expenditures of education and economic services accounted for 23.7% and 16.6%, respectively. The wages of employees in subvented organizations[22] and pensions were also raised. Overall, total expenditure and net lending rose by 45.7% in 1992, much of which represented an increase in the wage bill of 62.1% over the previous year. (Leite et al, 2000: 30–36).

Along with the general salary increase, the PNDC also granted large transfer payments to households in the last quarter of 1992. This occurred in the form of payouts of accumulated retirement and end of service gratuities that had been frozen since 1990 (Leite et al, 2000: 36). Bowing to the demands of public enterprises and subvented organizations, the Government agreed towards the end of 1992 to a program to encash accumulated retirement gratuities or end-of-service benefits. (Leite et al, 2000: 37).

There were delays in tax revenue collection during this period as well, resulting in a decline in tax collection from 12.4% of GDP in 1991 to less than 11% in 1992 (Leite et al, 2000: 30; Ghana's Budget, 1993: 2) (see Table 4.2). The weak tax administration led to a reduction in petroleum taxes, corporate tax rates, and in sales and excises taxes. (Leite et al, 2000: 36).

The domestic banking system also resorted to increasing borrowing (by as much as 30% even though the IMF conditions targeted a 22% decrease) (Leite et al, 2000: 30; Ghana's Budget, 1993: 2). Most of the money borrowed was used on rural development projects. According to Green (1995), the PNDC as part its election strategy launched a National Electrification Scheme in 1992, extending electricity to the countryside, though the project was actually announced in 1989. In 1992, Green notes that 100 towns and villages were added to the national grid, as were roughly 20 district capitals. Other dispensed rural patronage included water supply, feeder roads and school construction and improvement (Green, 1995: 578–580). The combined effect of these developments was an increase in the broad money supply of 51%, much higher than the IMF target increase of 12% (Ghana's Budget, 1993: 2).

As a consequence of these unprogrammed fiscal and monetary policies, the budgetary balance switched from a surplus equivalent to 1.8% of GDP to a deficit of 177 billion cedis (or 4.9% of GDP) (See Tables 4.2 and 4.3). Put another way, Ghana's overall balance of payments recorded a deficit of $124 million in 1992, as against the IMF's targeted surplus of $140 million.

NONCOMPLIANCE (3): JULY 1996-NOVEMBER 1996

Government and political developments and noncompliance activity by the PNDC

In a pledge addressed as much to anxious donors as to Ghanaians, President Rawlings vowed not to repeat the profligate pre-election budgetary management of 1992. Speaking before the parliament on January 18, 1996, he said: "Some observers . . . have assumed that since this is an election year, the government will relax control of economic management in order to pander to sectional interests. Let me assure . . . we have no intention to subordinate the nation's economic interests to political expediency. . . . We shall pursue our policies and programs with increased vigor and follow up our promotion of private investment." That pledge was restated three weeks later by Ghana's finance minister, Kwame Peprah.[23] When presenting the 1996 budget, Peprah said: "we do not intend to play election year politics with the economy . . . we have to take responsible actions and that in spite of electoral year risks, our responsibility to the longer term interests of our people must remain supreme." (Ghana's Budget, 1996: 1 & 42)

Notwithstanding these pledges, the PNDC was noncompliant with IMF conditionality during the second half of 1996 (in the run up to the elections) and experienced large fiscal overruns. Below are details of 1996 fiscal slippages.

The PNDC government exceeded its capital expenditure budget in 1996 by almost 78 billion cedis (Ghana's Budget, 1997: 5) though IMF conditionality called for a sharp reduction in capital outlays to 3.9% of GDP from 6% in 1995 (with road construction programs taking the biggest cuts).[24] Most of the increase in capital spending, however, went to the rural areas. For example, unbudgeted capital spending on rural roads in 1996 amounted to 0.5% of GDP. (Leite et al, 2000: 39).

Indeed, the total budgeted expenditure for 1996 was exceeded by 20%, with all major categories of expenditure exceeding their projected amounts (Bank of Ghana Annual Report, 1996: 23).

Noncompliance was also reflected in the PNDC's delay in petroleum tax collections. A system set up, in June 1996, to automatically adjust retail petroleum prices for variations in the price of imported oil was suspended, in September 1996, when it became evident that the adjustments lead to price increases. (Leite et al, 2000: 39). Overall, petroleum excise duties in 1996 was 17.2 billion cedis short of the IMF target of 300 billion cedis. (Ghana's Budget, 1997: 4)

Table 4.3. Central Government Budgetary Operations and Financing (as percentage of GDP)

	1990	1991	1992	1993	1994	1995	1996	1997	1998	1999
Overall balance (commitment basis)	-2.2	-1.3	-9.4	-9.9	-8.9	-6.4	-9.5	-10.3	-8.1	-8.2
Net change in domestic arrears	0.4	0.3	0.3	0.2	0.2	1.0	-0.1	-0.6	-0.6	-0.6
Overall balance (cash basis)	-1.8	-1.0	-9.1	-9.6	-8.7	-5.3	-9.6	-10.9	-8.7	-8.0
Divestiture receipts	0.0	0.0	0.0	2.1	4.9	1.4	1.3	0.7	0.6	0.3
Total financing	2.2	1.3	8.7	7.4	3.8	4.0	8.4	10.1	8.1	7.8
Foreign (net)	3.6	3.3	3.5	6.2	4.5	4.3	3.7	4.6	3.1	2.5
Borrowing	5.2	4.9	5.1	7.9	6.7	6.8	7.5	8.3	6.6	5.8
Project loans	2.4	2.8	3.5	4.9	6.2	4.9	5.4	7.7	5.3	4.7
Program loans	2.9	2.0	1.5	3.0	0.6	2.0	2.1	0.6	1.2	1.1
Amortization	-1.7	-1.5	-1.5	-1.7	-2.2	-2.5	-3.9	-3.7	-3.5	-3.7
Domestic (net)	-1.4	-2.0	5.1	1.2	-0.7	-0.4	4.7	5.5	5.0	5.3
From banking system	-1.0	-2.0	3.7	-0.6	-0.9	-0.9	2.0	3.7	2.0	5.1
From nonbanks	-0.4	0.0	1.5	1.7	0.1	0.5	2.7	1.7	2.3	0.1
Memoranda										
Domestic primary balance	0.1	1.8	-4.9	-3.2	0.8	1.5	0.3	3.2	3.6	1.4
Primary balance	-0.9	0.3	-7.3	-6.4	-4.4	-2.1	-4.4	-4.0	-1.1	-2.6

Source: IMF

As a consequence of these unprogrammed fiscal and monetary policies, the government's domestic primary surplus fell from 1.5% of GDP in 1995 to 0.3% in 1996, (see Table 4.3) leaving virtually all debt servicing to be financed by new credit. The recourse to credit led money supply to grow by 38%, although under the IMF terms, the annual rate of money supply growth was planned to fall from almost 40% at the end of 1995 to 5% by the final quarter of 1996.[25]

The IMF reacted to PNDC's noncompliance by quietly suspending its Enhanced Structural Adjustment Facility (ESAF) disbursements in October 1996. It was not until 18 months later, on March 23, 1998, that the IMF agreed to resume its annual loan under ESAF (IMF Press Release No. 98/8).[26]

NONCOMPLIANCE (4): JULY-DECEMBER 2000

Government and Political Developments and Noncompliance Activity by the PNDC

As it did in 1992 and 1996, the government again pledged to resist the temptation to pursue irresponsible expansionary fiscal policies during the 2000 election year.[27] Presenting the 2000 budget to parliament, Kwame Peprah, the finance minister, said: "we must resist the temptation to play political football with the economy in an election year. Populist demands, populist rhetoric, blackmail threats, wild cat strikes all combined to wreak havoc on the progress of our economic forward march during the two previous elections in 1992 and 1996." (Ghana Budget, 2000: 83).

Despite the verbal commitments to tighten fiscal policy, the government, again, succumbed to electoral pressures and relaxed fiscal discipline by boosting expenditure spending in the second half of 2000 and veering the IMF program "sharply off track."[28] The PNDC, in the second half of 2000, was noncompliant with IMF conditionalities in the following ways.

The wage bill and wage related payments exceeded IMF targets. In mid-May the government awarded a 20% across-the-board civil service salary increase, backdated to April 1, 2000. Polytechnic teachers were also granted a 20% salary increase in September. The salary increases pushed the fiscal deficit in 2000 to 6.9% of GDP, instead of the IMF target of 4.2%.[29]

The ceiling on net domestic financing of the government was also missed by a wide margin. Recourse to domestic bank, rather than expenditure restraint, doubled reserve money growth, from 18% (annual rate) at end of June 2000 to 36% by end of 2000. Indeed in December 2000, none of the fiscal and monetary targets were met.[30]

As summarized by the IMF, "weak fiscal and monetary policies at the end of 2000, prior to elections, had led to a rise in inflation, a substantial depreciation in the exchange rate, a decline in foreign exchange reserves, and a significant rise in domestic and foreign debt as a share of GDP."[31]

The PNDC's troubles with the IMF were further compounded when the government fudged economic data to IMF officials in August 2000, in order to meet IMF targets, and secure its annual loan. Much of the facts surrounding this incident is still shrouded in secrecy, but here is what we know. On June 28, 2001, the IMF fined the Ghanaian government $39 million for misinformation given by the previous government covering the last quarter of 2000.[32] Following the Funds decision to fine Ghana, the Deputy Managing Director and Acting Chairman of the IMF, Eduardo Aninat, without revealing the precise nature of misinformation, stated:

> The reporting of inaccurate information took place under the previous government. The new government has been very forthcoming and cooperative throughout the inquiries into these problems and has taken steps to prevent future occurrences, including stricter procedures for authorizing external borrowing and enhanced monitoring of external debt payments. . . . The Board concluded that waivers of nonobservance of the prior action and performance criterion could not be granted, and Ghana was asked to repay the noncomplying disbursement, together with any interest accrued thereon."[33]

The IMF official resident stationed in Ghana, Brayden Kemp, was a little more expansive. He said: "The precise motive is something that we are not able to determine after the fact, especially since the governor of the Bank of Ghana at the time is no longer in office. . . . I think people can draw their own conclusion about why they might have wanted to understate the rate of monetary growth at a time when monetary supply was in fact growing very rapidly."[34]

CONCLUDING ANALYSIS

PNDC Chairman Rawlings embraced the logic of IMF fiscal conditionality wholeheartedly, at least verbally. Seeking to "dispel some of the inevitable misunderstandings about IMF conditionalities," Rawlings affirmed that IMF conditionalities "[are] simple economic common sense." He explained: "Nobody has to tell us, for example, that in an agricultural organization with 49 tractors and over 500 tractor drivers, some of those drivers must be deployed elsewhere" (The Ghanaian Chronicle, April 19–25, p. 12). If IMF conditionalities are 'simple economic common sense'" to Rawlings, what explains his regime's four major noncompliance activities, outlined above? In accordance with the analytic framework developed in Chapter 1, the factors that would take a borrowing country into noncompliance are the governments assessment of high political costs, which may result from elite instability proxied by four variables: plots, attempted coups, coup d'etats, and forced resignations (Morrisson and Stevenson, 1971) and/or elections.

ELITE INSTABILITY AND NONCOMPLIANCE

As illustrated above, the end of 1995 and early of 1986 marked a difficult period in Ghana's compliance with IMF conditionalities. In a confidential memo prepared for Ghana in October 1986, the IMF acknowledged that the slippages in policy implementation during this period had threatened to undermine the country's economic recovery. Indeed, in mid 1986, the PNDC came close to abandoning the adjustment program altogether.[35]

The historical survey of the political events during that period (outlined above) indicates that the high degree of political agitation and elite instability, as evidenced in the numerous coup attempts, coup plots and the vociferous labor demands, broke the PNDC's resolve to remain faithful to IMF conditionality. Moreover, the Ghanaian population was, during this period, showing signs of what has been called "adjustment fatigue."[36] The TUC-led opposition to the PNDC's compliance with the IMF conditionalities, together with the intensified attempts at overthrowing the PNDC regime, created a very precarious political environment, one which led many senior PNDC officials to predict the regime's collapse by the end of May 1986.[37]

That the political survivability of the PNDC was a deciding factor in the PNDC's decision to become noncompliant with IMF conditionalities in 1986 is summed up in the words of PNDC Chairman Rawlings himself. Explaining why his regime conceded to labor demands, he expressed the belief that labor, at that time, had been infiltrated by the U.S. Central Intelligence Agency (CIA) and other "enemies of the revolution," bent on overthrowing his regime. Rawlings said:

> "Now, taking the security situation on a broader perspective, I want you to know that the government has been aware of the infiltration of the labor front by dissident forces who see the labor front as a weak and easily manipulated link in trying to destabilize the process—this,

> of course, having failed to achieve what they had set out to do on the military front. Now, the ignorance of the labor front has been unduly capitalized on and it was considered strategically important to concede to the workers in order to prevent the disgrace they would have suffered as a result of their low-level consciousness."[38]

He explained further that:

> Individuals within the labor front and others with close links, we know, had been plotting and planning for some time. There are so many instances—I don't think I am going to go into deeper details. But as we know, they quickly capitalized on a situation where they could manipulate the rest of the workers by preying on their ignorance and, shall we say, selfish personal sentiments. Now, this action, as I was trying to indicate, should not be isolated from the recent revelations about mercenaries and guerrillas preparing to move in with arms, ammunition from Argentina to throw the whole process back. And I am glad that our people have wised up and suspected a situation like this, so that we don't have to come out trying to say it to be doubted by the people, but I am glad they are drawing these conclusions themselves. . . . Now, let me go beyond our domestic front—the CIA we have been talking about is a very powerful organ with exposed orchestrators and actors who do not move on only one front, but they move on several fronts.[39]

It is very revealing from the above that the regime during the period in question believed its political survival to be on the line and had to neutralize labor agitation by reneging on IMF compliance. The deteriorating domestic political situation also made the IMF more flexible in their conditional demands. As Martin Matthew noted, "by September [1986], the Fund's board saw the PNDC was having major political problems and softened the program," in particular by agreeing to the second exchange rate auction arrangement. (Martin, 1991: 249)

ELECTIONS AND NONCOMPLIANCE

Our period of study leads to one clear conclusion: elections promoted noncompliance in the form of fiscal laxity. Manipulating fiscal policy, in developing countries, has proven to be an effective means of influencing government popularity in election years. In a study of 24 developing countries, Ludger Schuknecht (1998: 155–170) found that fiscal policies, because they have an immediate effect on voters well-being for which governments can claim direct credit, are an oft used election tool. He also found that the favorite opportunistic fiscal policy for vote-seeking governments in the developing countries was public spending. He explained that "public spending increases are the preferred vehicle for policy makers to boost their popularity before elections because they typically have a very direct and immediate impact on voters' welfare." (Ludger Schuknecht, 1998: 155). Schuknecht goes on to argue that, because developing countries have a small tax base, election-oriented policy-making is more likely to occur in the form of (capital and current) expenditure increases rather than tax reductions. Ghana's second, third, and fourth noncompliance activities (outlined above) mirror Schuknecht's conclusions.[40]

During election years, Rawlings' government, with its political future on the line, threw out the economic rationality of IMF conditionality and spent its way to hold on to power.

Both the IMF and the PNDC acknowledged that Ghana's economic adjustment program had been sacrificed for political purposes in 1992. A 1996 confidential report prepared for Ghana by the IMF conceded that the PNDC had found it difficult to maintain an anti-inflationary fiscal policy stance during the transition to multiparty democracy due to the overriding considerations given to securing the acquiescence of the labor unions in the public sector. The PNDC also admitted that "virtually all expenditure items recorded excesses over [IMF's] programmed levels" in 1992 (Ghana's Budget, 1993: 2) but argued that noncompliance was justified in order to maintain a stable political and social environment during the critical transition to constitutional rule. At the proceedings of the meeting of the consultative Group for Ghana held in Paris on June 24 and 25, 1993, Finance Minister Kwesi Botchwey argued that Ghana's successful transition to democracy was not without its costs and that the direct costs of elections proved to be larger than anticipated. Botchwey went on to tell the donor countries that the pay hike demanded by civil servants in 1992 was particularly hard to ignore given the inherent merit of their demands and, more importantly, given the urgent need to secure the social and political environment for a successful political transition. Botchwey argued further that the strength of the support for Rawlings, particularly in the rural areas where poverty is most prevalent, gave the people's verdict on the ERP.[41]

Botchwey's argument that the increases in expenditure (i.e., noncompliance) were necessary to maintain social peace is interesting as it speaks to the issue of political stability, the inverse of elite instability. As Kuznets writes "some minimum political stability is necessary if members of the economic society are to plan ahead and be assured of a relatively stable relation between their contribution to economic activity and their rewards"

(1966: 451). But maintaining social peace during an election period is a strategic objective to achieving one's ultimate political goal: retaining power. As Ninsin noted: "on the eve of competitive electoral politics in 1992, the logic of political survival and self-succession heightened the value of regime legitimacy for the Rawlings government and drove it to embark on more public spending on rural and community development projects regardless of the negative effect of uncontrolled public spending on the public budget" (Ninsin, 1998: 198).

The government's fiscal noncompliance of 1996, like that in 1992, was directed at achieving election victories. According to Ninsin, Rawlings and his party won the 1996 elections because "the electorate perceived them as the ones who control the scarce resources needed for the development of their communities . . . [and] the ones with demonstrable capacity and commitment to either deliver or punish communities that do not show sufficient support at the polls" (Ninsin, 1998: 199).

It must be noted that the strategy of legitimating a government or regime through massive expenditures is not foolproof and could be counter-productive. As Wright (1978:157) has argued: "there is a certain logic to legitimation which means that the political apparatus gets progressively diminishing returns in added legitimation for a given program over time. Once a program becomes seen as right, the continuation of the program adds little to the legitimacy of the state where as a cutback in the program would constitute a source of delegitimation." However in the case of Ghana, where the vast majority of voters are peasants, illiterate, and live in closely knit communities, it is plausible to expect the electorate to respond positively to the politics of patronage because voting usually represents the collective interests of the community, and not of the individual per se. Ninsin reminds us that:

> "the majority of Ghanaians have, usually, voted neither to express individual political preferences, nor as autonomous citizens of the state acting in association with other autonomous citizens to choose a government and thereby influence, howbeit indirectly, the direction of future policies of the country. People have voted as part of a political collective—the community—to register either their collective appreciation for material benefits like development projects (a road, clinic, electric power, piped water, a school block, etc.) received in the past." (Ninsin, 1998: 196).

It appears the IMF is seeing the links and connections between elections and fiscal outruns. Writing on Ghana, the IMF noted that "elections may encourage politicians to spend unwisely in an attempt to impress voters" (IMF, 2000:1).

Chapter Five
Conclusion: Lessons on Compliance and Conditionality

"The problem is that economists most of the time treat the policymaker as a machine that can be programmed [however] once the right policy has been singled out, it is up to the policymaker machine to implement it."

—Edwards and Tabellini (1991: 16)

INTRODUCTION

This study has presented a comprehensive analysis of the unevenness in compliance with IMF conditionality in Ghana under the PNDC. The first chapter of the study presented a review of the literature relevant to the research problem and specified the analytic framework employed in the study. The second and third chapters presented a comprehensive examination of the political economy of Ghana's compliance with IMF conditionality by tracing the historical factors that have shaped compliance, identifying the various actors in Ghana impacted by IMF conditionality, and examining the political strategies used by the PNDC to enforce conditionality. Specifically, I established in these chapters that association with IMF and/or compliance with IMF conditionalities have historically been a highly sensitive political issue in Ghana (beginning with the Nkrumah government). However, given the country's free falling economy, Rawlings felt he had no choice but to go to the IMF for assistance. To ensure compliance with conditionalities, Rawlings shifted his allegiance away from students, labor and radicals, (his initial support base) who apart from lacking political power lacked an alternative vision to IMF conditionality. He subsequently embraced the national elite and clamped down, in heavy-handed fashion, all opposition to conditionalities. Chapter 4 recounted IMF conditionalities during 1983 to 2000 and identified periods of non-compliance and the prevailing political factors prior to each non-compliance period.

This chapter, as a conclusion to the study, has the following objectives: to restate the research problem and key findings; to go beyond the data and make propositions with regard to the relationship between elections and elite instability on the one hand and compliance and conditionality on the other; and to situate the Ghanaian experience within the broader context of IMF conditionality in Sub-Saharan Africa (SSA). Throughout this chapter, I point to newer issues for which I believe further research and analysis are necessary.

RESTATEMENT OF RESEARCH PROBLEM AND KEY FINDINGS

The central objective of this study, as set out in the introductory chapter, was to achieve a greater understanding of Ghana's compliance with IMF conditionality. The central theoretical questions that informed this study were: a) When and why do recipient governments deviate, even if only temporarily, from the terms of IMF conditionality? Why do some adjusting countries, while complying with loan conditions, adopt policies that have the effect of neutralizing or undermining SAPs? In essence, the central question was: What causes an adjusting government to risk a rupture in its SAP, and thus its relationship with the IMF?

I identified the survival drive and desire of a political regime to maintain political power as a major explanatory factor on why noncompliance with IMF conditionality occurs. I argued that two such critical moments when there is a need to muster domestic support in order to stay in power (and when we can expect noncompliance) are periods prior to elections and periods of elite conflict/instability.

A. Hypothesis one: Elite instability-induced noncompliance

Here, I argued that the support of the political elite is key to the survival of any political regime, democratic or otherwise, thus any form of inter-elite violence, be it a coup, alleged plots, or forced resignations creates high political cost for the political regime. To increase the probability of staying in power, the regime would become noncompliant with IMF conditionality by embarking on unprioritzed expenditure policies in order to garner more support (or equivalently reduce opposition) from the population, or at least its key constituents.

The findings

This hypothesis was confirmed, if somewhat tentatively, by our analysis of the data. Specifically, the political violence/instability, expressed in the forms of coup attempts, labor strikes and dissident activity, crested in the first quarter of 1986, and influenced the PNDC's decision to make strategically important concessions to workers, leading to noncompliance with IMF wage conditionalities.[1]

B. Hypothesis two: Pre-election noncompliance

Here, I argued that although IMF conditionality typically constrains discretionary expenditure policies, incumbent governments seeking to boost their popularity and re-election chances would be noncompliant with IMF conditionality by embarking on opportunistic policy-making prior to elections.

The findings

This hypothesis was confirmed, resoundingly, by our analysis of the data. Specifically, the elections of 1992, 1996, and 2000 influenced the government's decision to violate IMF conditionalities. As shown in the preceding chapter, with overriding considerations given to securing the support of the labor unions and rural voters, Rawlings' PNDC granted substantial large salary increases and embarked on unprioritized rural capital spending prior to elections.

SUMMARY OF THEORETICAL AND POLICY IMPLICATIONS

Several observations, on the question of compliance and conditionality that have potential theoretical and policy implications flow from these findings:

1. The State in Africa

In terms of theory, the first cluster of findings, from this project, deals with the literature on the contemporary state in Africa. Numerous African analysts, in typical Weberian approach, have equated state autonomy with state strength and capacity. The state is portrayed as strong and autonomous on the basis of its ability to realize its own internally generated interests at the expense of civil society.[2] Our observation (deduced from Chapter 3) cautions against making such generalizations that cast the relationship between state and societal actors in zero-sum terms. Based on the findings of this study, the relationship between state autonomy, strength and capabilities cannot be described uni-dimensionally. I will then agree, theoretically, with Migdal (1987: 396) that it is necessary to move away from abstract typologies (of 'strong' and 'weak' states) that simply pit state against society. The state is part of society and is embedded within the network of social (as well as class) relations that define its characteristics, not the atomized structure as some theories of the state postulate.[3]

In terms of policy, our findings suggest that the Fund, when drawing up conditionalities, ought to move away from its statist paradigm and embrace a state-society perspective. As our study has demonstrated, when conditionalities are drawn up by the Fund and negotiated with recipient countries, there is a tendency to design them on the basis of a monolithic state, ignoring the various dimensions of the internal decision-making structure. There is also the inherent presumption of an autonomous state devoid of social pressures. This poses a paradox in that many governments (like Ghana's) are coalitions of parties and individuals that may have different views about conditionalities (see Chapter 3).

While our study on Ghana established that compliance is a matter of state choice, it also suggested that the state is not a unitary actor, unaffected by the influences of vested interest groups. A broad political economy perspective, to analyze who the winners and losers of conditionality are, and how strong they are, is therefore necessary to explain compliance and non-compliance. In other words, one important precondition for avoiding non-compliance with conditionality is that the different constituents in the society should be identified and their relative power and independence as regards policy-making taken into account. In Ghana's case we established that the national elite, or those who occupy echelon and strategic positions in the economic and social structure, such as senior or top persons in the military or labor, are most important. The PNDC's concessions to labor, in spite of conditionality, is particularly noteworthy in this study. Consequently, the Fund, if it seeks to improve the compliance rate of its programs, ought to design conditionalities that are politically as well as economically viable.

2. Regime Type

Our second set of findings deals with a thorny issue in the politics of adjustment literature: the question of whether some political systems are better suited to enforce compliance than others. The central issue at the heart of this debate is the question of whether authoritarian regimes are better suited to enforce compliance with conditionalities, or conversely, whether conditionalities themselves are politically destabilizing in ways that elicit authoritarian responses (Haggard, 1985: 509).[4] In other words, is there a relationship between compliance/noncompliance, repression and authoritarianism? The evidence has been mixed.

Those who hold that authoritarian regimes are better suited to enforce compliance and sustain adjustment[5] argue that distributional coalitions (i.e., social groups or organizations for collective action that have little incentive to make sacrifices) are so strong in democracies that they constrain the policy autonomy of government. Thus, only strong authoritarian measures can control these coalitions and enforce compliance.[6] Others however, like Nelson (1984) and Remmer (1986), have challenged the notion that authoritarian regimes are better suited to enforce compliance with conditionalities. According to Nelson et al. (1990: 8), "there is no one correlation between economic gains and political support; much depends on how the gainers fit into existing political institutions and processes." So while Stone (2002) reported that authoritarian countries are more likely to become noncompliant, Stephan Haggard (1985) found no correlation between regime type and the ability to comply.[7]

This study's historical analysis of Ghana (1983–2000) does not confirm a strong causal link between ability and willingness to comply and any particular political system such as democracy or authoritarianism. As Chapter 4 indicated, noncompliance under Rawling occurred during both the democratic and authoritarian phases of his regime. We should hasten to add, however, that within the democratic setting, the risk of the government losing power through the ballot box made prediction of noncompliance more certain. The IMF appears to agree with this study's findings: noncompliance occurs during build up to elections. In its Occasional Paper series on Ghana in 2000, the IMF said:

> "a democratic environment and a participatory approach to economic policies are no panacea. Consultation and consensus building can (and do) delay policy implementation. The strategies chosen sometimes involve too many compromises or are too timid. Protection of minority rights and interests can be overlooked under the guise of majority rule. Consultations with stakeholders can become perfunctory and fail to really take their views into consideration. Deadlocks may halt reforms, and elections may encourage politicians to spend unwisely in an attempt to impress voters." (IMF, 2000: 1).

The broader implication of this finding is that compliance with conditionalities are more likely to be successful when a few skilled technocrats make economic policy, as happened in Ghana in the mid-1980s. While the decision-making process was undemocratic during the authoritarian phase of Rawlings' regime (1983–1992), it was successful in ensuring compliance. What is interesting is that Rawlings' regime had roughly the same amount of years (eight) as an authoritarian regime (1983–1992) as it did as a democracy (1992–2000). Yet, three of the noncompliance activities occurred within a democratic setting (prior to elections) and only one noncompliance activity occurred within the authoritarian phase of Rawlings' regime.

It is one thing for the Fund to be cognizant of the problem of noncompliance prior to elections, and it is yet another thing for it to do something about it, which leads us to our third observation: the issue of moral hazard.

3. Moral Hazard

The third set of observation points out that continued IMF program lending, in spite of noncompliance, induces moral hazard by the recipient country.[8] Moral hazard is defined as the undue risk-taking behavior of investors and creditors who are reassured because the government can be counted on to intervene in case of a major financial shock.[9] As it applies to conditionalities, member countries (creditors), pursue risky behavior (noncompliance) but do not fear the consequences of punishment, and are rather confident that the IMF will save them by providing more financial assistance (Vaubel, 1983).

The case of Ghana shows that 'recidivism' sets in if noncompliance with conditionalities goes unpunished. As shown in the previous chapter, noncompliance with conditionalities was met with very brief and temporary withdrawal of aid, followed by further IMF negotiations and assistance. Several reasons have been advanced to explain why the IMF did not discontinue its conditional lending to Ghana given the country's early noncompliance with conditionalities.[10] Factors cited include: the PNDC's track record; the speed and rigor with which it implemented conditions; the difficulties and failure of other adjustment efforts in SSA; and the improvement in broad macroeconomic indicators, including GDP growth; and the budget and current account deficits. Factors which indicated to the Fund that aspects of the PNDC's adjustment program were working.[11]

From a macroeconomic point of view, there was good reason for the IMF and other donors to view Ghana's adjustment as favorable. As the before-after comparison of broad macroeconomic indicators in Table 5.1 reveal, improvements in the economy began to take hold after the adoption of conditionalities.

Table 5.1. Ghana: Changing Economic Performance

	1965–73	1973–80	1980–88
GDP Growth	3.5	-0.5	2.0
Inflation rates (CPI)	6.4	60.3	43.0
Export Growth	0.4	-8.7	3.2
Import Growth	-7.8	-3.6	3.8

Source: World Bank, Trends in Developing Countries, 1990

Jay Oelbaum, (2002: 316) even wrote that the superlatives showered on Ghana's program by the IMF was so profound that opposition leaders were unaware of Ghana's program difficulties with the IMF during the 1990s.

But what consequences does continued program lending, despite noncompliance, have on a star candidate (like Ghana), and what impact do further rounds of negotiations and subsequent loan approval for that country have on potential Fund clients? This is not a mere academic question but one with real empirical consequences. The fact is that inconsistent or uneven compliance negates the economic gains that occurred in the country prior to noncompliance (as happened in Ghana during the periods after noncompliance, particularly in 1992 and 1996), and continued program lending may adversely affect the country's reputation in the international capital markets, and leave it dependent on further loans and more conditionalities (Bird, 2002).

For potential Fund clients, the availability of Fund support, despite noncompliance, might encourage them to pursue risky loans (i.e. passively accepting IMF conditionalities without securing firm domestic commitments) in an attempt to get "something for nothing."

If the IMF wants better compliance with its conditionalities, then it should perhaps consider the ex-ante conditionality proposed by Vaubel (1983), and more recently by the Meltzer Commission (IFIAC, 2000), for all its loan facilities.[12] The "ex-ante conditionality" thinking argues that it is difficult for member countries to adhere to Fund conditionalities since they are imposed after the member country has gotten into balance of payments difficulties. Thus, IMF loans should only be given to countries that have taken preventive measures aimed at minimizing the risk of a crisis erupting. Nations that have negligently, or even deliberately, created a precarious economic situation should be barred from receiving IMF loans all together. Ex-ante conditions could, for example, include a requirement that domestic credit expansion may not exceed the growth of production potential or that the budget deficit may not exceed a certain percentage of the gross national product (Vaubel, 1983).

4. Selectivity and sensitivity

The fourth observation is that some conditionalities are more politically sensitive than others. In Ghana, the common denominator of all conditionalities that precipitated noncompliance was the wage bill. The first noncompliance with conditionalities, in April 1986, occurred as a concession to worker demand for wages. The 1992, 1996, and 2000 noncompliance all involved the granting of large salary increases to workers prior to elections (see preceding chapter for details). Since Ghana's noncompliance occurred mainly in the form of wage concessions, it provides an important lesson that greater selectivity has to be applied when designing conditionalities with an eye to ensuring that real wages does not decline significantly. It also implies that unsustainable wages in the presence of a well-organized labor force could result in political expression. This is particularly significant since the IMF maintains that it is committed to sustainable (but not excessive) wage rates.[13]

5. Measuring noncompliance

The fifth and final observation of this study has to do with the operationalization of the dependent variable itself: Compliance and noncompliance are not easily quantifiable frames. While this study employed a very specific metric for measuring noncompliance (a violation which warranted IMF intervention or reprimand), it became evident that there is a whole spectrum of possibilities rather than a singular or one-dimensional phenomenon that can be empirically measured as noncompliance. As shown in Chapter 3, currency devaluations (as an IMF condition), for example, may foster exports but offset trade liberalization or policies designed to achieve price stability, thus making it impossible to meet broad targets set by the IMF. Moreover, it is quite possible for noncompliance to be undetected, due to selective disclosure and reporting or unreliable data (an example of this occurred in Ghana's 2000 noncompliance, see Chapter 4).

Theoretically, this means there is no one metric utilized for assessing relative compliance or noncompliance and further work may be warranted in this regard. In terms of policy, greater efforts must be made to develop reliable and sound monitoring and data capacities.

THE FUTURE OF CONDITIONALITY AND AFRICA'S COMPLIANCE

In this concluding section, I widen the scope of our findings to the rest of Africa to provide a political explanation of why the Fund has not had much compliance success with African countries. I will argue that the evolving nature of conditionalities to include 'country ownership' and the political realities of instability and demands for elections throughout Africa do not augur well for compliance.

EVOLVING CONDITIONALITY

Conditionality has evolved substantially over the history of the Fund. While the use of IMF resources has involved policy conditions since the mid-1950s, formal guidelines were not developed until 1968. In 1979, the Guidelines on Conditionality was issued to underscore the principle of parsimony and the need to for the Fund to pay due regard to a member country's social and political objectives, economic priorities, and circumstances.[14]

Since 1999, with the introduction of PRSPs,[15] the Fund has sought to foster the concept of a country's "ownership" of a program in order to increase the borrowing government's sense of responsibility for the conditionalities and ensure compliance and program success.[16] The logic is that 'ownership' matters because it positively influences commitment to reform. The reverse logic is that noncompliance occurs because programs are perceived as Fund imposed and not serving the best interests of the borrowing country. Horst Köhler, IMF's then newly appointed Managing Director, stated that ". . . The Fund is streamlining conditionality with the objective of promoting greater ownership and strengthening the implementation of programs."[17]

On September 25, 2002, the Executive Board formally approved a new set of guidelines on conditionality (replacing guidelines that had been in effect since 1979) where a member country's reform agenda would be drafted as much as possible by the local authorities rather than by Fund staff.

But just what 'ownership' means remains ambiguous. After much internal debate, the Fund defined ownership as "a willing assumption of responsibility for an agreed program of policies by officials in a borrowing country who have the responsibility to formulate and carry out those policies, based on an understanding that the program is achievable and is in the country's own interest (IMF, 2001: 6).

There are a number of problems with the IMF's emphasis on ownership in conditionalities. First, the concept of ownership, as it now reads, is poorly operationalized. It is not hard to agree on the conceptual statement of ownership in principle, but it is very difficult to know where to draw the line in practice between countries whose conditionalities are owned and ones that fall short since ownership is neither static nor directly observable. For instance, what bridge does a country have to cross to signal to the IMF that its program is owned? Under what condtions will the Fund justify loan refusal on the basis of non-ownership?

The second, and more important, problem with the IMF's new direction is that the very idea of ownership is prima facie incompatible with conditionality. The fact is that conditionalities (as our study has shown) are usually not in the political interests of borrowing countries. If it were, countries would implement the appropriate reforms on their own volition, without the Fund conditionalities, hence owning the reform process without the need for Fund conditionalities. It is precisely because of the incompatibility between conditionality and ownership that noncompliance occurs. Indeed the whole idea of owning conditionalities is tautological. How can the policy conditions negotiated in exchange for loans be "owned" by the borrower? At the end of the day borrowing countries under this 'new' model, will still not have much choice and autonomy to pursue whatever policies that they (the borrowing country) wish; they will continue to adopt policies that meet the benchmarks and guidelines approved by the IMF. If African governments, and borrowing countries for that matter, are to reacquire primary responsibility for defining and implementing their economic policies they cannot do so by exercising such an initiative in tandem with IMF (and other donor) conditionalities under the guise of "ownership." African governments, the IMF, and other actors, should perhaps listen to the counsel of Joseph Stiglitz, then the World Bank's chief economist (who resigned—in part due to disagreement over the Bank's continuing use of conditionality). When asked whether conditionality was an effective way of changing national policies, he said: "There is increasing evidence that it was not. Good policies cannot be bought."[18] A future focus of research on whether the IMF's new emphasis on ownership in conditionalities has impacted compliance is warranted.

THE PROSPECTS OF COMPLIANCE IN AFRICA

Africa has experimented with IMF conditionalities for the last twenty years, yet it is a region that has not made much progress with the conditionalities that the IMF encourages.[19] The implications of our study to the rest of the region make clear why noncompliance with IMF conditionalities has been prevalent and why more of the same can be expected. The first has to do with the Africa's endemic political elite instability (this study's first independent variable). Between 1990–2000, there were 25 successful coups and 71 coup attempts in the 53 countries, an average of 1.33 attempted coups per country, or about 6.5 per year.[20] Obviously, a successful coup means a greater likelihood of noncompliance, since new regimes in Africa usually interrupt Fund conditionalities. Augustin Fosu reminds us that "the African historical coup incidence record is replete with accounts of emerging military coup leaders decreeing new rules such as debt abrogation, cancellation of previous currency devaluations and reinstitution of government subsidies" (Fosu, 2002: 332). As we outlined in Chapter 3, such policies, while they tend to favor the political elite go against the assumptions of IMF conditionalities.

But even if political elite instability were not an issue, our second independent variable, prior election spending, can explain why noncompliance with IMF conditionalities has been, and will continue to be, an issue for the Fund. A quick and brief survey of the literature on IMF programs in Africa show a correlation between elections and noncompliance in SSA: Kenya exceeded the ceilings on bank credit to the government during July-December 1979, prior to presidential elections in November of the same year (Killick 1983: 401); Tanzania's IMF program was suspended in August 1975 for pre-election profligacy (Cline, 1983); Sierra Leone (in April 1982) and Zaire (in June of the same year) had their programs cancelled prior to elections. (Haggard 1985: 514); Burkina Faso's program was cancelled between presidential elections in December 1991 and parliamentary elections in May 1992 (Diabré, 1999). Similar problems occurred in Guinea, Kenya, Mauritania, Senegal, and Togo (Mecagni, 1999: 223). Though these examples are not cited from comprehensive studies linking elections to noncompliance, taken together with our findings on Ghana, they do expose a clear pattern of a strong correlation between the two variables.

Moreover, the idea of "liberal democracy" where political leaders regularly compete for power through free and fair elections is now a fact taking hold in Africa. Around 100 elections had taken place in Africa between 1989 and 1994,[21] and four out of every five African countries held multiparty elections in the 1990s. While we are not suggesting that prior election noncompliance took place in all African countries with IMF programs, we are raising the prospect that difficulties with conditionalities, such as those experienced in Ghana, are likely during election periods. Moreover, multiparty elections have now become an important political conditionality for IFI's as they deal with certain African countries; the case of Zimbabwe being a recent example.[22]

The above analysis shows that compliance with IMF conditionalities will continue to be an issue in Africa. First, with an increase in conditionalities, it is more probable that a country will fail to comply fully with all of them. Second, our assumptions of the political elite (that they are selfish and would use all available resources to stay in power) imply that politicians are likely to be noncompliant when their survival is at stake.

Though this study centered on just two variables (elections and political elite instability) in the rational choice considerations, there are certainly other crucial variables in the political market that may affect noncompliance. The notion of political sovereignty as a variable may be explored further (see Chapter 2). For example, a pro-IMF government that is accused of selling out the country by the opposition (or by some members of the coalition) might become noncompliant as a way to affirm the country's independence and defacto sovereignty and soothing nationalistic fears.

Also, while our study has shed light on the domestic political variables that may affect compliance, work of this type needs to be done within the IFIs as well to uncover what mix of domestic and international political institutions and variables allow for better adherence to conditionalities. Edwards' (2001) study on the effect of variables representing international power and influence on the suspension of IMF programs due to noncompliance found that the Fund was less likely to suspend a program in countries with larger quotas. The implication is that the IMF may treat larger states differently because of their impact on world economic activity, or alternatively, the IMF may keep lending to larger states in order to maximize its own expenditures and attain some bureaucratic goal. Stone (2002) also analyzed the IMF's lending credibility, and found that countries that have the support of foreign supporters such as the U.S. are more likely to be noncompliant and have more inflationary policies but are subject to shorter periods of IMF program suspension. Such research findings are important because discovering the combination of political variables at different levels of analysis would make our prediction and explanation of noncompliance richer.

It is possible to analyze compliance and noncompliance with conditionalities in a strictly technical way, discussing administrative and technical capacities, etc. (Weiss and Jacobson 1998). But what our study has shown is that the political economy behind them, such as the power of social groups as well as election politics, is more interesting and important to understand the phenomenon of compliance. The IFI's will do well to pay heed to these variables.

Notes

NOTES TO CHAPTER ONE

1. See Harold James, International Monetary Cooperation Since Bretton Woods (New York: Oxford University Press, 1996), for a history of the international monetary system; and A. F. P. Bakker, International Financial Institutions (London: Addison Wesley, 1996), for a survey of IFIs.
2. Recent years have seen a proliferation in IFI conditionalities, with politically related conditionalities, such as 'good governance' gaining more prominence. For example, since 1996, the World Bank has begun over 600 governance-related programs and initiatives in 95 countries and is involved in supporting significant programs of governance and public sector reform in 50 countries (Santiso: 2001: 3). For a good background on political conditionality, see Kapur and Webb (2000). For an excellent summary of the changing scope of IMF conditionality, see Jacques J. Polak, "The Changing Nature of IMF Conditionality," Essays in International Finance, No. 184, Princeton University, 1991; and Guitian, Manuel (1995), "Conditionality: Past, Present, Future: Celebrating Fifty Years of the International Monetary Fund."
3. John Williamson (1993) refers to IFI conditionality in biblical terms, referring to conditionality as "Ten Commandments" of reform and arguing that although not always the same everywhere, these "Ten Commandments" provide the benchmark for IFI conditionality. The list reads as follows: remove import quotas, cut tariffs, reduce taxes, adjust interest rates, curb public borrowing, reduce subsidies, liberate multinational corporations, divest public enterprises, retrench civil service, and rewrite regulations on business.
4. Economic growth is the percentage increase in real national output in a given time period or a sustained increase in the productive potential of an economy (World Bank 1995).
5. This study is concerned only with IMF policy conditions.
6. The actual provision of IMF loans is linked to a government's implementation of a program of specific policies. The conditions are specified in a

"Letter of Intent" signed at the initiation of a program by the recipient country.

7. There exist various forms of conditionality, including preconditions or prior actions as well as trigger actions which determine continued access to development financing and the next outstanding installments of loans. The various aspects of IMF conditionalities will be discussed as this study progresses.
8. Although compliance with conditionality is not legally enforceable, the IMF may limit or withhold the further disbursements of loans if a country violates the terms of its loan conditionality. Overall, member compliance with IMF conditionality tends to be mediocre despite the lure of financial assistance and a chance to improve economic performance. (Doe 1983, Haggard 1995, Bird 1998).
9. An adjusting country is one that has undertaken SAP with an IFI.
10. There is too ample a body of literature on conditionality to pay justice to it in this paper. Most have dealt with the impact of conditionality. The record, however, remains mixed. A selected sample of case studies would include Tony Killick, IMF Programmes in Developing Countries: Design and Impact (London: Routledge, 1995). Bird Graham, The International Monetary Fund and Developing Countries: A Review of the Evidence and Policy Options. International Organization (summer): 477–511. 1996.
11. Gold, Joseph Gold (1972), Voting and Decisions in the International Monetary Fund (Washington DC: IMF); Kapur, Devesh (2000), "Who Gets to Run the World?," Foreign Policy, No. 121, November/December 2000: pp. 44–50; and Van Houtven, Leo (2001), Governance of the International Monetary Fund: Decision Making, Institutional Oversight, Transparency and Accountability (Washington DC; Per Jacobssen Foundation).
12. See Alexander Wendt, 'Anarchy is What States Make of It,' International Organization, 46/2, 1992; Finnemore, Martha, National Interests in International Society, Cornell University Press, 1996, Ch. 1, (pp. 1–33) and Checkel, Jeffrey, "The Constructivist Turn in International Relations," World Politics 50 (2), January 1998 (pp. 324–348).
13. I am mindful of the fact that their arguments dealt mainly with treaties. However, the themes and premises they present are transferable to state agreements with IIs.
14. For a discussion on the limitations of the PA model to IMF conditionality see Killick (1997).
15. We are not assuming that retaining political power is the only goal of politicians but we are implying that it is a major goal.
16. Élites are those who get the most of what there is to get in the distribution of values in a society and who hold authoritative positions in the institutions governing the distribution of the values they hold (Stevenson 1971: 346).
17. Conflict is defined as a condition in which participants in a social relationship hold incompatible or mutually exclusive values (Stevenson 1971: 348). Political violence is behavior characterized by the physical injury or subjugation of persons or property with the intent to bring about an alteration in the structure of the political system.

18. Retrospective voting implies that "votes are cast on the basis of economic performance, rather than economic policy proposals" (Lewis-Beck 1988, 40).
19. The literature on economic voting argues that economics matter: "when economic conditions are bad, citizens vote against the ruling party" (Lewis-Beck, 1991: 2). Thus economic conditions are associated with the popularity—or lack thereof—of elected governments. Beck finds in Western Europe that popular support for the incumbents falls with economic downturns. Therefore, in the politics of these countries, economics matter (Lewis-Beck 1988: 22). He finds that "evaluations of collective economic performance and policy move the voter. In particular, in each of these nations retrospective and prospective evaluations of government economic management significantly influenced incumbent support" (Lewis-Beck 1988, 156). Several other studies, such as those of Kramer (1983), Kiewiet (1983), and Markus (1988) also find a relationship between national economic performance and the vote for incumbents.
20. Authoritarianism is defined as "a government where one political party maintains control through force and/or propaganda, or where there is no political party, with control maintained by one or more persons. Elections, if they are held, are meaningless" (Dick 1974: 818).
21. We are concerned here with inter-elite conflict, as opposed to violence of the elite (or government) against the masses (Rummel 1976). A more precise definition of this phenomenon is provided on pages 27 and 29 of this study.
22. See Sklar (1979), The Nature of Class Domination in Africa, Journal of Modern African Studies, December 1979, 531–552. Also Irving Leonard Markovitz (1977). "The Consolidation of Power: The Rise of the Organizational Bourgeoisie." In Power and Class in Africa, pp. 199–229.
23. The amount by which total government spending is more than government income during a specified period; the amount of money which the government has to raise by borrowing or currency emission in order to make up for the shortfall in tax revenues.
24. It is also important to note that IMF conditionality usually hurts all those groups who are net beneficiaries of the budget deficit (that is those who receive direct payments and transfers from the government, such as public officials, the military, and police).
25. This is an illustrative study, and hence we are not suggesting that a single case study will answer the question of why states become noncompliant definitively. The aim here is to establish the plausibility of our hypothesis, using the Ghanaian case, and then broadening our universe of study once our findings are confirmed. In other words, treating Ghana as the empirical case should not obscure the broader objective of this study. This objective is to explore the policy implications on the issue of noncompliance with IMF conditionalities that promise to evolve out of a theoretically informed empirical study.
26. For more of "within case" analysis, see Alexander George, "Case Studies and Theory Development: The Method of Structured, Focused Comparison," in

Paul Gordon Lauren, ed, Diplomacy: New Approaches in History, Theory and Policy, New York, Free Press, 1979.

27. The Fund makes payments to the central bank of an adjusting country, and not to government ministries or officials. The Bank of Ghana is the central bank of Ghana.
28. On November 22, 1999, the IMF's concessional facility for low-income countries, the Enhanced Structural Adjustment Facility (ESAF), was renamed the Poverty Reduction and Growth Facility (PRGF), and its purposes were redefined.

NOTES TO CHAPTER TWO

1. As we indicated in Chapter 1, the political elite are those who get the most of what there is to get in the distribution of values in a society and who hold authoritative positions in the institutions governing the distribution of the values they hold (Stevenson 1971: 346). We identify the characteristics and social groups that come under the political elite category in Chapter 3.
2. See subsequent pages for more on his socialist leanings.
3. For useful and concise accounts of the Ghanaian economy, see Abbey in John Loxley, Ghana: Economic Crisis and the Long Road to Recovery, The North-South Institute, Ottawa, 1988; Szerezewski R, Structural Changes in the Economy of Ghana, Weidenfeld and Nicolson, London, 1965; W. Birmingham, I. Neustadt and E.N. Omaboe (eds.), A Study of Contemporary Ghana: Volume 1—The Economy of Ghana, Allen and Unwin, London, 1966; Killick T, Development Economics in Action, St. Martin's Press, 1978, and J.C. Leith, Foreign Trade Regimes and Economic Development: Ghana, Columbia University Press, New York,1974.
4. In a sense, Nkrumah was a product of his times: In the 1950s and 1960s the state was viewed by economists, aid donors, and multilateral organizations as a capable economic agent (Herbst, 1990: 951).
5. Irving Markovitz tells us, however, that Nkrumah's polices toward domestic private business enterprises did not lead to a decrease in private enterprise, but rather an increase. Irving Leonard Markovitz, Power and Class in Africa (Englewood Cliffs: Prentice Hall, 1977), p. 257.
6. Export finance, which is available to a supplier of items as distinct from credits to the foreign purchasers under buyer's credit. These are normally covered by Letters of Credit/ Bank Guarantees arranged for a short-term period, usably up to six months.
7. Andrzej Krassowski, Development and the Debt Trap: Economic Planning and External Borrowing in Ghana (London: Overseas Development Institute, 1974), 42.
8. The Fund's legal authority is based on an international treaty called the Articles of Agreement (Articles or the Agreement) which came into force in December 1945. Article I(v) purports "to give confidence to members by making the general resources of the Fund temporarily available to them under adequate safeguards, thus providing them with opportunity to correct

maladjustments in their balance of payments without resorting to measures destructive of national or international prosperity." See Bird, Graham. 1994. "The Myths and Realities of IMF Lending." World Economy 17 (5): 759–778. Ghana also consulted the World Bank later that same year.

9. Prior actions are measures that a country agrees to take before the Fund's Executive Board approves a loan and before the initial disbursement takes place. Such measures ensure that the program has the necessary foundation to succeed.
10. *Osagyefo* (an Akan word) means the "warrior."
11. Hass (1998: 18) distinguishes between deliberate compliance, when states adhere to international obligations and serendipitous compliance when states' actions fit or conform to international obligations, but without a deliberate choice.
12. For more on the principles guiding IMF operations and how that is antithetical to economic nationalism, see Laurence Harris, "conceptions of the IMF's role in Africa." In Peter Lawrence (ed), World Recession and the Food Crisis in Africa. (London: James Curry, 1986). Pp. 83–87.
13. For more on the 1966 coup see: Afrifa, Akwasi A. The Ghana Coup. London: Cass, 1966.
14. General Joseph A. Ankrah was called from a forced retirement to head the new government of the National Liberation Council (NLC). The military coup itself was executed by Afrifa and Kotoka. Kotoka was killed in a counter-coup attempt by two lieutenants on April 17, 1967.
15. The International Monetary Fund announced on February 23, 1967 that it had concurred with a proposal by the Ghana Government to replace its existing currency unit, the cedi, with a new unit to be called the new cedi, one new cedi being equivalent to 1.2 old cedis. It was stated that the change would come into effect immediately; would not involve appreciation or depreciation of Ghana's currency; and would make the par value for the new cedi 1.24414 grammes of fine gold or U.S. $1.40, equivalent to 0.714286 new cedi per U.S. dollar.—(IMF, Washington).
16. Busia appeared to be torn between the role of the state and market in economic development. Berating state intervention in economic policy-making Busia said: "state ownership and control of economic enterprises leads to concentration of both political and economic power in the hands of those who are governing, [and] men who come to have such power [will] use it to enrich themselves, to deny employment to others, to arrest others [and] to have their own way (Busia: 1966). Yet at the same time he maintains that the state has a critical function in economic development. This led Tony Killick to remark of Busia's economic program: "In spite of an apparently positive attitude to the free operation of market forces, a large role was also envisaged for the state" (Killick, 1978: 56).
17. This policy of purposeful defiance became known in Ghanaian political circles as "Yentua" (literally meaning "we won't pay").
18. In response to an oil crisis, the IMF created an Oil Facility in 1974, and enlarged it in 1975, to aid members in balance of payments difficulties.

19. In 1975 Acheampong replaced NRC will an all military Supreme Military Council (SMC).
20. The Financial Times, July 4, 1979.
21. M. M. Huq broadly defines *Kalabule* (the then newly coined word in Ghana) as a parallel market economy that "covers all types of illegal transactions including smuggling of cocoa, timber and gold; diversion of goods from official to unofficial channels; tax evasion and over-invoicing of imports and under-invoicing of exports." (Huq, 1989: 309).
22. For other accounts of the negotiations and conditions between the Limann government and the Fund see: The Financial Times (London), January 27, 1982, Ghana: An Economic Tragedy, pp. 14, and The Economist, January 9, 1982, Ghana's Black Star, p. 40.
23. New York Times, June 7, 1981. Ghana's Leader Asks U.S. Aid for Ailing Economy. p. 8.
24. Ibid.
25. The Economist, January 9, 1982, Ghana's Black Star, p. 40.
26. Accra Domestic Service in English, "Commentary Rejects any Devaluation of Cedi," March 2, 1982, reprinted in Joint Publications Research Service, Sub-Saharan Africa (JPRS, SSA), 17 March 1982, 36.
27. Ministry of Information. J.J. Rawlings, Selected Speeches vol. 3. Accra, Ghana: Ministry of Information, 1990. p. 18–19.
28. "Policy Guidelines of the PNDC." Accra: Information Services Department. Restricted Document. May 1982 (preface).
29. Provisional National Defence Council, Policy Guidelines For Ministries and Regional Organizations. Restricted Document. May 1982. p. 2.
30. Confidential Interview, Washington DC, May 24, 2003.
31. Confidential Interview, May 2003.
32. PNDC Two Years. (Accra: Information Services Dept. 1984). Pp. 24–25.
33. Financial Times (London), January 5, 1983. Also, Africa Research Bulletin, December 15-January 14, 1983, p. 6690.
34. Much of the discussions on the PNDC and IMF negotiations are not fully sourced because they are based on confidential interviews and confidential IMF materials.
35. K. Ewusi (1988) Equity Implications of the Stabilisation and Adjustment Programmes in Africa: The case of Ghana. Cambridge, England.
36. H. Tabatabai: Adjustment Policies and Access to Food in Ghana, in International Labour Review, ILO, Geneva, Vol. 127, #6. p. 706.
37. John Williamson and Stephan Haggard, "The Political Conditions for Economic Reform," in Williamson, The Political Economy of Economic Reform (Washington: Institute for International Economics, 1994) p. 565. For more on economic crises and reform see Alberto Alesina and Allan Drazen, "Why are Stabilizations Delayed?" American Economic Review 81(5) (1992): 117088; Allan Drazen and Victorio Grilli, "The Benefits of Crisis for Economic Reform," American Economic Review 83 (3) (1993): 598607. Raúl Laban and Federico Sturzenegger, "Distributional Conflict, Financial Adaptation, and Delayed Stabilizations," Economics and Politics

6 (3) (1994): 25776; and "Fiscal Conservatism as a Response to the Debt Crisis," Journal of Development Economics 45 (2) (December 1994): 305–24.

38. Radio and TV Broadcast to the Nation. Thursday July 29, 1982, in "Selected Speeches of J. J Rawlings" v.1. p. 42.
39. Radio and TV Broadcast to the Nation. December 31 1983, in Selected Speeches of J. J Rawlings" v. 2 p. 65.
40. John Dunn eloquently makes this point in Modern Revolutions (New York: Cambridge University Press, 1972), p. 12–22.
41. We will discuss the stakeholders and the politics of adjustment, in depth, in Chapter three.
42. West Africa, January 13, 1986, p.69.
43. An editorial in its paper, The Workers' Banner, September 16–23, 1982.
44. Relations with Cuba and Libya, for example, were normalized nine days after the coup.
45. Yeebo, interview by author, August 5, 2003.
46. Kwame Amoah was appointed PNDC's Secretary of Finance, only to have the appointment retracted two hours later.
47. Graham, interview by author, August 4, 2003.
48. "Report of the Committee of the National Defence Committee and the Secretaries on the Economy." Accra: Information Services. September 10, 1982.
49. "IMF Again. . . . We Disagree," The Workers' Banner, September 16–23, 1982.
50. Speech by Rawlings at the National Seminar on an Economic Recovery Strategy. January 19, 1983. In Selected Speeches of J. J. Rawlings," v. 2, part II p. 3–4.
51. Radio and TV Broadcast to the Nation. May 2, 1983, in "Selected Speeches of J. J Rawlings" v.2 p.17.
52. The importance of the secrecy of these IMF meetings should not be lost, because even people very close and loyal to the PNDC "revolution" were not in the loop on all the IMF contacts prior to the April 21 1983 budget statement. The first Secretary for Youth and Sports in the former PNDC, Zaya Yeebo, for instance, writes, erroneously, that the PNDC began negotiating with the Fund to secure loans in February 1983 (Yeebo, 1991:117). Zaya Yeebo resigned and went into exile shortly after the budget statement.
53. As noted earlier the NERC comprised mainly of technocrats who saw some form of compliance with IMF conditionality as a prudent way to deal with the country's fiscal and BOP problems.
54. People's Daily Graphic, May 20, 1983.

NOTES TO CHAPTER THREE

1. We use co-optation here to mean "a process of absorbing new elements into the leadership or policy-determining structure of an organization as

a means of averting threats to its stability or existence." Philip Selznick (1966: 13).

2. For detailed discussions of the history and nature of the African state, and the politics therein, see N. Chazan, R. Mortirner, J, Ravenhill and D. Rothchild, Politics and Society in Contemporary Africa (Boulder: Lynne Rienner, 1992), ch. 2; C. Charney, Political Power in the Neo-Colonial African State, Review of African Political Economy, Vol. 38 (April 1987); J. F. Medard, The Underdeveloped State in Africa: Political Clientelism or Neo-Patrimonialism?, in C. Clapham, ed., Private Patronage and Public Power (London: Pinter Printers, 1982); and Markovitz Irving Leonard, Power and Class in Africa (New Jersey: Prentice Hall Press, 1977) ch. 6.
3. Diamond, Larry (1987) Class formation and the swollen African state. The Journal of Modern African Studies. 25, no. 4 (567–596). p. 70.
4. Diamond, op cit.
5. These elite categories expand on Max Assimeng's (1996: 40) conception of the Ghanaian elite by specifying lawyers, large land owners as well as traditional rulers.
6. For a short and concise summary of the classical elite theorists–Pareto, Mosca, Burnham, and other—see Parry (1969: 30–63).
7. See also Markovitz, 1977: 153–172.
8. Of course, interest differentiation exists among this national elite, but the majority view is presented here for simplicity.
9. For an account on how exchange rate was used to benefit the national elite and a means of developing and retaining constituencies in Ghana see Report of the Commission of Enquiry into Alleged Irregularities and Malpractices in Connection with the Issue of Import Licenses (Akainyah Commission) (Accra: Government Printer, 1964), 12; and Report of the Commission of Enquiry into Trade Malpractices in Ghana (Abraham Commission) (Accra: Government Printer, 1965). Also Herbst "Exchange Rate Reform: Strategy and Tactics" in Herbst, Jeffrey. The Politics of Reform in Ghana, 1982–1991. Berkeley: University of California Press, 1993.
10. W. Adda, "Ghana," in Privatization in Developing Countries, ed. V. V. Ramanadham (London: Routledge, 1989), 305.
11. Daniel Swanson and Teferra Wolde-Semait, Africa's Public Enterprise Sector and Evidence of Reforms, World Bank Technical Paper no. 95 (Washington, D.C.: World Bank, 1989), 31.
12. Robert M. Price, "Neo-Colonialism and Ghana's Economic Decline: A Critical Assessment," Canadian Journal of African Studies 18, no. 1 (1984): 188.
13. Quoted in Kojo Yankah, The Trial of Rawlings (Accra, 1986) p. 17.
14. Interview with Zaya Yeebo. Former PNDC secretary. August 6, 2003.
15. See "Provisional National Defence Council (Establishment) Proclamation, 1981." January 11, 1982. In Laws of the PNDC v. 1. Laws 1–12. Accra: Information Services). P. 5–14.
16. A Roman Catholic priest, Rev. Dr. Damuah had been criticized by the former government of Dr. Hilla Limann for attacking exploitation of Ghanaians by the ruling elite.

17. Joachim Amartey Kwei was a noted Labor activist.
18. With the possible exception of Rawlings whom analysts have variously described at the time as been "open-minded" (Rothchild, 1991: 160), non-ideological (Hutchful, 2002: 51), pragmatic (Aryeetey et al, 2000: 44).
19. Yeebo. Interview. August 10, 2003.
20. See J. J. Rawlings, "First Year of Holy War" Radio and TV broadcast to the Nation on Thursday, December 16, 1982, in Selected Speeches. p. 80–90.
21. Yeebo. Interview. August 10, 2003.
22. See Daily Graphic, February 17, 1982; and Agyeman Duah (1987: 620).
23. In a sign of the internal rift between the regime leadership, Mr. Chris Bukari-Atim, a member of the PNDC and chairman of the Interim National Coordinating Committee (INCC, set up to supervise and co-ordinate the work of the PDCs and also the recently established workers' defence committees—WDCs), the following day, criticized attacks on the committees by 'counter-revolutionary chiefs and so-called big men.' This was a veil, if undisguised, reference to Rawlings since Rawlings had attacked the people's defence committees (PDCs) for removing managers and heads of commercial organizations from their posts without any clear evidence of malpractice. See Jerry Rawlings, "Revolutionary Potentials of PDCs," Radio and TV broadcast to the nation to mark May Day, Saturday, May 1, 1982. In selected speeches of J.J. Rawlings, 1982 p. 27.
24. Marketing manager of the State Fishing Corporation.
25. Chairman of the interim management committee of the Maritime and Dock Workers Union.
26. A traditional chief of Namdam in the Northern Region of Ghana.
27. A retired appeals court judge and the then president of the national Olympic committee.
28. She had held ministerial office from 1961 to 1966 under President Kwame Nkrumah.
29. Yeebo. Interview by author. August 10, 2003. The PNDC had normalized relations in Libya, a country that was considered a pariah state not only by the West but also by ECOWAS (Economic Community of West African States). Most of ECOWAS including Ghana under Limman, had severed diplomatic relations with Libya over the latter's subversive actions in Chad and throughout the sub-region. (West Africa, June 7, 1982, p. 1550).
30. See "Resisting Injustice" Radio broadcast to the nation. Thursday December 31, 1981. In selected speeches of J.J. December 31, 1981–December 31, 1982 p. 1–3.
31. 'No more empty theories," West Africa, September 2, 1983. p. 14.
32. Radio and TV Broadcast to the Nation, August 23, 1983.
33. Interview, West Africa, December 24, 1984.
34. The details of IMF conditionalities are specified in Chapter 4.
35. The structure of Ghana's banking system is as follows: At the top is the Central Bank (The Bank of Ghana); followed by the Primary Banks (Ghana Commercial Bank, Standard Chartered Bank and Barclays Bank); Secondary Banks (Social Security Bank, National Savings and Credit Bank, Bank of Credit and Commerce, Agricultural Development Bank, National

Investment Bank, Bank for housing and Construction, Merchant Bank, and Ghana Cooperative Bank) . The Rural Banks are at the base of this pyramid.

36. Organized non-governmental associations.
37. Yeebo. Interview. August 6, 2003. See also Ofuatey Kodjoe, 1998: 184.
38. For accounts on the labor movement in Ghana see: Panford, Martin Kwamina, IMF-World Bank and Labor's Burdens in Africa: Ghana's Experience (Westport, Conn.; London: Praeger, 2001); Jon Kraus, "Strikes and Labour Power in Ghana," Development and Change 10, no. 2 (April 1979); Richard Jeffries, "The Labour Aristocracy? Ghana Case Study," Review of African Political Economy, no. 3 (May–October 1975): 68–69; Jeff Crisp, The Story of an African Working Class: Ghanaian Miners' Struggles, 1870–1980 (London: Zed Books, 1984); E. A. Cowan, Evolution of Trade Unionism in Ghana, Accra: 1970.
39. The ILO conventions governing these rights are ILO Convention No. 87 (Convention concerning Freedom of Association and Protection of the Right to Organize), and ILO Convention No. 98 (Convention concerning the Application of the Principles of the Right to Organize and to Bargain Collectively).
40. Richard Jeffries, Class Power and Ideology in Ghana: The Railwaymen of Sekondi (Cambridge: Cambridge University Press, 1978), 197.
41. Jon Kraus, "Strikes and Labor Power in Ghana," Development and Change 10, no. 2 (April 1979): 281.
42. At the time of the ERP, the TUC was made up of 17 affiliated unions. The most important are the Ghana Private Road Transport Union (GPRTU), Ghana MineWorkers' Union, and the Railway Workers' Union. In 1991, total membership of the TUC was over 650,000 workers (Kraus, 1990).
43. This caused a significant number of workers, particularly those stationed in the Accra–Tema metropolitan area to support an alternative, radical trade union center, the Association of Local Unions (ALU), "whose leaders advocated overthrowing the TUC bureaucracy altogether and were linked with the June Fourth Movement" (Jeffries, 1991: 161).
44. The Pioneer, September 21, 1984.
45. A. K Yankey, How Ghana's Labour Movement Sees the IMF. Lagos Guardian (Nigeria) (December 1985), p.10.
46. N. Bentsi-Enchill, "Paying the Price," West Africa, 13 January 1986, p. 78.
47. Ghana budgets covering these periods.
48. Details of IMF conditionalities are outlined in Chapter 4.
49. Republic of Ghana, Consultative Group Report, 1986–1988, Accra. p.30.
50. Republic of Ghana, "Enhancing the Human Impact of the Adjustment Programme," Report for the Sixth Consultative Group, Accra, April 1991. p. 39.
51. op.cit, p.40.
52. U.S. House of Representatives, 1989, "Structural Adjustment in Africa: Insights From Experiences in Ghana and Senegal," Report to the Committee on Foreign Affairs, Staff Study Mission To Great Britain, Ghana,

Senegal, Cote d'ivoire and France, November 29–December 20, 1988, U.S. Government Printing Office. p. 6.

53. COCOBOD was the largest parastatal at the time.
54. The Pioneer, November 5, 1984.
55. Transcript, Ghana: Workers protest against TU leaders." BBC Summary of World Broadcasts, June 8, 1987.
56. Transcript, "Ghana: miners' strike ends, union leaders sacked." BBC Summary of World Broadcasts, August 18, 1987.
57. After an extensive public education campaign, the VAT was re-introduced in 1998 (at a lower level of 10% compared to the 15% recommended by the government).
58. Hi-Ed News, The NUGS viewpoint, March 1992.
59. The students' support dated back to Rawlings' June 4, 1979 uprising when they had been more radical and to the left of the AFRC.
60. Yeebo, Interview by author, August 10, 2003.
61. Ghanaian Times, August 29, 1987.
62. West Africa, August 17, 1987.
63. Hi-Ed News, The NUGS viewpoint, March 1992.
64. The universities reopened in October 1984, more than a year after it had been closed.
65. The police were on the campus to enforce the government order.
66. Transcript, "Ghanaian Government Closes University over Student Dispute." BBC Summary of World Broadcasts, May 11, 1987
67. BBC, op. cit.
68. NUGS statement 1983.
69. For a treatment of the ethnic and temporal differences in the Ghanaian army see Jean Allman "Imagined martial communities: recruiting for the military and police in colonial Ghana, 1860–1960" in Ethnicity in Ghana: the limits of invention by Carola Lentz and Paul Nugent. New York: St. Martin's Press, 2000. See also, The Ghana Army: A Concise Contemporary Guide to its Centennial Rregimental History, 1897–1999 by Festus B. Aboagye. Accra: Sedco, 1999, and Politicians and Soldiers in Ghana, 1966–1972 by Dennis Austin and Robin Luckham, London: Cass, 1975, for the politics of the Ghanaian army.
70. Ghanaian Times, June 5, 2003.
71. Transcript, "The Military Coup in Ghana: address by Rawlings." BBC Summary of World Broadcasts January 4, 1982.
72. "Conditionality in the International Monetary Fund," by Ross Leckow—IMF Seminar on Current Developments in Monetary and Financial Law. Washington, D.C., May 7, 2002. (Unpublished paper) p. 6.
73. Yeebo, Interview by author, August 10, 2003.
74. A new investment law, the Ghana Investment Promotion Center Act, 1994, Act 478, was passed in November 1994 to replace the Investment Code of 1985, then the most comprehensive business legislation. The law reestablished the Ghana Investment Center under the new name of the Ghana Investment Promotion Center, but with the same singular aim:

"to encourage and promote investment in the Ghanaian economy." The 1994 Act differed in certain respects from the Investment Code of 1985, in that the functions of the Center now include: The initiation and support of measures that will enhance the investment climate for both Ghanaian and non-Ghanaian companies; promotion of investment in and outside Ghana through effective promotional means; and offering advice, upon request, on the availability, choice, or suitability of partners in joint venture projects. While, under the 1985 Code, the chairman, vice-chairman and members of the Board of the Center and the chief executive were appointed by the then government, the Provisional National Defence Council (PNDC), under the 1994 Act, it is the president who, in consultation with the Council of State, appointed members of the Board.

75. The Investor. Ghana Investment Center, v. 1, no.1 (October–December 1990), p. 5–8.
76. See C. Atta Mills, Structural Adjustment in Sub Saharan Africa. World Bank-EDI Seminar Report # 18, (Washington DC: World Bank, 1989) PP. 21–23.
77. Yeebo, Interview by author, August 10, 2003.

NOTES TO CHAPTER FOUR

1. Most IMF loans are disbursed in phases. This allows the IMF to verify that a country is adhering to its commitments before disbursing successive installments. Program monitoring relies on prior actions (measures that a country agrees to take before the Fund's Executive Board approves a loan and before the initial disbursement takes place), performance criteria (conditions that have to be met for the agreed amount of credit to be disbursed), and program reviews (annual or semi-annual, broad-based assessment by the Executive Board of progress with the program).
2. See Margaret de Vires, The IMF in a Changing World, 1986, pp. 221–222. Also, Miles Kahler, "Orthodoxy and its Alternatives: Explaining Approaches to Stabilization and Adjustment," in Joan Nelson (ed) Economic Crisis and Policy Choice, (Princeton: PUP, 1990) pp. 38–39.
3. See Joseph Gold, Stand By Arrangements. Washington D.C. IMF, 1970. pp. 3–5.
4. See "Extended Fund Facility." Decision No. 4377-(74/114) in Selected Decisions of The Executive Board, 1991. pp. 105–109. See also, Miles Kahler, "Orthodoxy and its Alternatives," 1990. p.42; Margaret de Vires, 1986, pp. 222.
5. IMF website, http://www.imf.org/external/np/exr/glossary/index.as (Cited May 20, 2003).
6. The Fund has recently (2002) instituted two new facilities, the Supplemental Reserve Facility (SRF) and Contingent Credit Lines (CCL). The SRF provides assistance for exceptional balance of payments difficulties due to financial market crises. The CCL was instituted for countries that are

concerned about the possible fallout of a financial market crisis, and want credit to be available if needed.

7. As of January 2002.
8. Republic of Ghana, Economic Recovery Programme, 1984–86 v.1. 1983, Paris and Accra, pp. 12–13.
9. Republic of Ghana, "PNDC Budget Statement and Economic Policy for 1987." Accra, 1987. p. 5.
10. Republic of Ghana, "PNDC Budget Statement and Economic Policy for 1987." Accra, 1987. p. 5. See also Dordunoo and Nyanteng, 1997.
11. For more on conditionality, see: Collier, P., P. Guillaumont, S. Guillaumont and J.W. Gunning (1997), Redesigning conditionality, World Development, 25(9), September. Isham, Jonathan and Daniel Kaufmann (1995) 'The Forgotten Rationale for Policy Reform: the Productivity of Investment Projects,' World Bank Policy Research Working Paper No. 1549. Washington, DC: World Bank, November, and Killick, Tony with Ramani Gunatilaka and Ana Marr (1998), Aid and the Political Economy of Policy Change (London: Routledge and Overseas Development Institute).
12. Daily Graphic, February 2, 1985.
13. Noticias Argentinas (1513 GMT), March 18, 1895; BBC Summary of World Broadcast (0700 GMT), June 23 1986.
14. "Swap In Spy Cases Made With Ghana," The New York Times, November 26, 1985, p.6; "Ghana, swap and diplomatic expulsions," United Press International, November 30, 1985.
15. Ghanaian Times, January 21, 1986. p.2.
16. "Ghana; Adjustment fatigue Sets In," Financial Times, May 20, 1986, p. 15.
17. Some facts in what follows in this chapter are not fully sourced because they are based on confidential IMF and World Bank documents and confidential interviews.
18. Confidential Interview, Washington. August 2003. The point is also confirmed in confidential IMF and World Bank documents.
19. The IMF condition for resuming talks was that the PNDC agree to rescind part of the salary increase, which it did on June 1, 1986.
20. Finance Minster Kwesi Botchwey in defending the wage roll back denied IMF pressure. He said: "It is not a question of the Fund pushing us. It is our own wages and incomes policy, and our own objectives for investment growth and inflation, which are in question. The excess in the wages bill is inconsistent with ERP II, which is investment-orientated. These increases are consumption-orientated." (Ghana; Warning Over Income Levels, Financial Times, May 20, 1986, p. 20).
21. The new two-tier foreign exchange auction was introduced by the PNDC on September 19, 1986.
22. Subvented agencies are independent agencies of government that receive subsidies from the budget to cover at least part (and often all) of their expenditures (Leite et al, 2000: 30–36).

23. Claiming frustration and fatigue, Ghana's long serving Finance Minister, Dr. Kwesi Botchwey, quit his post on July 11, 1995. Ethnic NewsWatch, The Weekly Journal, July 27, 1995.
24. Based on a confidential interview, and confirmed in "Ghana: African trail-blazer begins to falter: A lapsed recovery programme prompts concern about prospects for the continent as a whole." Financial Times, July 9, 1996, p. 5.
25. Confidential Fund document, 1997.
26. Coincidentally, the very same day, when Bill Clinton, the U.S. president, visited Ghana as the first stop of his 12-day tour of Africa.
27. Much of the official government economic activity data for the last quarter of 2000 is unavailable, and provisional where available.
28. IMF Country Report No. 01/141, August 9, 2001, p. 9.
29. IMF Country Report No. 01/141, August 9, 2001, p. 9.
30. IMF, op cit.
31. IMF Public Information Notice (PIN) No. 01/84, August 9, 2001.
32. On March 23, 2000, the IMF adopted rigorous policies, procedures, and remedies for addressing the misreporting of information to the IMF and proposals for strengthening safeguards on use of its resources. Stanley Fischer, Acting Managing Director, summarized the policy discussions: "Reliable information is essential to every aspect of the Fund's work—surveillance, financing, and technical assistance—and is particularly important in ensuring that the Fund's resources are used for their intended purposes. As has been the practice over many years, the Fund must depend primarily on trust in members' readiness to provide the information needed and to use the Fund's resources for the purposes envisaged. . . . While known incidents of misreporting and misuse of the Fund's resources have been rare, many Directors noted recent instances involving allegations of misuse of Fund resources and cases of misreporting, and emphasized the importance of preserving the integrity of the Fund's reputation as a careful and prudent provider of financial assistance to members. Directors agreed that these events further underscore the need to strengthen the Fund's existing safeguards on the use of its resources." IMF, "Selected Decisions and Selected Documents of the IMF," December 31, 2000. p. 4.
33. IMF Press Release No. 01/32, IMF Executive Board Reviews Noncomplying PRGF Disbursement to Ghana, June 28, 2001.
34. BBC News Online, Ghana 'misled' IMF, posted 6 February, 2002, 10:02 GMT, http://news.bbc.co.uk/1/low/business/1803198.stm (visited May 11, 2003).
35. Confidential Interview, Washington. August 2003. This is confirmed by Matthew Martin, Negotiating Adjustment and External Finance," in Donald Rothchild (ed) Ghana: The Political Economy of Recovery 1991, p. 249.
36. Financial Times (London, England) May 20, 1986.
37. "Lost Between State and Market: The Politics of Economic Adjustment in Ghana, Zambia, and Nigeria" in Joan Nelson, ed. Economic Crisis and Policy Choice: The Politics of Adjustment in the Third World (Princeton University Press, 1990), p. 280–281.

38. BBC Summary of World Broadcasts, April 25, 1986, Friday, Part 4 The Middle East, Africa and Latin America; B. AFRICA ; ME/8242/B/1.
39. Ibid.
40. See also, The Economist, Ghana as Economic Model Good, but not at Election Time. April 25, 2002, p. 46.
41. Rawlings also won in the Greater Accra Region, where NUGS, the TUC, and the middle-class opposition had been unsparing in their anti-PNDC attacks. The only regions that the NPP opposition received a majority vote in were the Ashanti Region and Eastern Regions. The NPP, after documenting alleged irregularities of the November 1992 presidential election boycotted the parliamentary elections held on December 29, 1992. For varying accounts and interpretations of the 1992 elections, see Jeffries, R. & C. Thomas. 1993. 'The Ghanaian Elections of 1992,' African Affairs 92, 368: 331–66; and Oquaye, M. 1995. 'The Ghanaian Elections of 1992: A dissenting view," African Affairs 94, 375: 259–75. http://www.imf.org/external/np/exr/glossary/index.asp. http://www.imf.org/external/np/exr/glossary/index.asp

NOTES TO CHAPTER FIVE

1. Rawlings Interview on the Ghanaian economy, BBC Summary of World Broadcasts, April 25, 1986, Friday, Part 4 The Middle East, Africa and Latin America; B. AFRICA ; ME/8242/B/1
2. For more on this, see Evans, Reuschemeyer and Skocpol (eds) Bringing the State Back In (Cambridge: CUP, 1985)
3. For a discussion of some recent theories of the state, see Raymond Geuss. 2001. "The State," in History and Illusion in Politics, Cambridge: Cambridge University Press, p. 14–68, Herbst, Jeffrey. States and Power in Africa. Princeton University Press, 2000; Migdal, Joel S. State in Society: Studying How States and Societies Transform and Constitute One Another, Cambridge University Press, 2001; and Barzel, Yoram. 2002. A Theory of the State: Economic Rights, Legal Rights, and the Scope of the State. Cambridge: Cambridge University Press.
4. For an earlier critique of IMF conditionalities along this line, see Cheryl Payer, The Debt Trap: The IMF and the Third World (New York: Monthly Review Press, 1974).
5. James Malloy, "Authoritarianism and Corporatism in Latin America: The Modal Pattern," in James Malloy, Authoritarianism and Corporatism in Latin America, (Pittsburgh, University of Pittsburgh Press, 1977) p. 3–19; and O'Donnell, Guillermo and Roberto Frenkel. 1980. "The Stabilization Programs of the IMF and their Internal Effects," in Richard Fagen (ed) 1980. Capitalism and the State in the U.S.-Latin American Relations, Stanford: Stanford University Press.
6. The concept of 'distributional coalitions' was developed by Mancur Olsen. See Mancur Olsen, The Logic of Collective Action (Cambridge: Harvard University Press, 1971).

7. In a latter work with Kaufman, Haggard refined this position, arguing instead that, "strong" authoritarian regimes insulate technocrats who design and administer economic reforms from societal pressures, thereby enhancing their capacity to carry out such changes; "weak" authoritarian regimes give less latitude to technocratic reformers who are subordinated to political elites and their pursuit of patron-client relations. Furthermore, they maintain, that "consultative" democracies are better at compliance than "plebiscitary" democracies or even authoritarian states. Haggard and Kaufman (1989: 233).
8. This section (on moral hazard) benefited from comments made by Graham Bird, who has a forthcoming article on the issue: Bird, Graham, Mumtaz Hussain and Joseph P. Joyce. 2004. "Many Happy Returns? Recidivism and the IMF." Journal of International Money and Finance, (forthcoming).
9. Prescott, Edward S. 1999. "A Primer on Moral-Hazard Models." Federal Reserve Bank of Richmond Economic Quarterly 85 (Winter): 47–77.
10. Killick et al (1998) asserts that noncompliance with conditionality goes unpunished for various reasons. Among these are the external pressures on donor agencies to continue aid, fears that withdrawal of aid will have destabilizing macroeconomic effects, as well as staff promotion criteria and accounting systems in the donor agencies that create powerful pressures to keep spending even when governments break their promises.
11. Confidential Fund Interview, Washington, May 28, 2003. Similar comments have been expressed by Dr. Ishan Kapur, Division Chief, West Africa in Daily Graphic, July 2, 1991. p. 1.
12. In November 1998, the U.S. Congress established the International Financial Advisory Commission (IFIAC), an 11-member panel headed by Professor Allan Meltzer of Carnegie Mellon University, as a part of legislation adding $18 billion to the U.S.'s capital contribution to the IMF. The assignment of the IFIAC, better known as the Meltzer Commission, was to study the role and effectiveness of seven international institutions (the International Monetary Fund, the World Bank Group, the Inter-American Development Bank, the African Development Bank, the Bank for International Settlements, and the World Trade Organization) and recommend future U.S. policy towards them. The Commission submitted its final report to the U.S. Congress and Department of Treasury on March 8, 2000, advocating substantial changes at multilateral development banks. The full report and subsequent updates can be viewed at http://www.bicusa.org/usgovtoversight/meltzer.htm http://www.bicusa.org/usgovtoversight/meltzer.htm.
13. IMF 1999, Transcripts on IMF seminar, "A Role for Labor Standards in the New International Economy?" Hampton Room, Omni-Shoreham Hotel Washington, D.C. September 29, 1999.
14. See Selected Decisions and Selected Documents of the International Monetary Fund, Twenty-Fourth Issue, Washington DC, 1999, pp. 137–139.
15. The Poverty Reduction Strategy Papers (PRSPs) are the most concrete and widespread manifestation of IMF/WB efforts to increase country ownership (see Chapter 3). As of March 2003, 51 out of 78 eligible countries had prepared either a preliminary paper ("interim" or I-PRSP) or a full

PRSP, and most of those had been approved by the Executive Boards of the Bank and the Fund as a basis for lending. Only 24 of those, however, were full PRSPs. (IMF website, http://www.imf.org, accessed March 2, 2003).

16. See, for example, Boughton, James M. and Alex Mourmouras. 2002. "Is Policy Ownership An Operational Concept?" IMF Working Paper No. 02/72. Washington, DC: IMF; and Khan, Mohsin S. and Sunil Sharma. 2001. "IMF Conditionality and Country Ownership of Programs." IMF Working Paper No. 01/142. Washington, DC: IMF.
17. International Monetary Fund. 2001. "Report of the Managing Director to the International Monetary and Financial Committee on the IMF in the Process of Change." Washington, DC: IMF.
18. Alan Beattie, "World Bank Aid Strategy Flawed Says Departing Chief Economist," Financial Times, November 29, 1999 (for quote); and "The Bumpy Ride of Joe Stiglitz," The Economist, December 18, 1999.
19. See for example, F. Noorbakhsh and A Paloni, Structural Adjustment Programs and Growth in Sub-Saharan Africa: The Importance of Complying with Conditionality," Economic Development and Cultural Change, Vol. 49 (2001), pp. 479–509.
20. Statistics on African coups provided by Dr. Randy Stone (University of Rochester) during The Yale Center for International and Area Studies' conference on "The Impact of Globalization on the Nation State from Above: IMF and Word Bank" April 25–27, 2003 at Yale University, New Haven Connecticut.
21. See "Elections in Africa" Royal Institute of International Affairs, Briefing Paper #2, April 2003, UK.
22. A large number of donors have recently scaled down or suspended their operations in Zimbabwe, citing the deteriorating political climate. The Executive Board of the International Monetary Fund (IMF) on December 3, 2003 initiated procedures to compulsorily withdraw Zimbabwe's membership, "after having determined that Zimbabwe had not actively cooperated with the IMF." (IMF Press Release No. 03/210, Washington DC, USA, December 3, 2003). Other donors and agencies have limited their activities to social concerns, including HIV/AIDS, social protection, and human rights. Websites: http://www.imf.org , http://www.bicusa.org/usgovtoversight/meltzer.htm, http://www.bicusa.org/usgovtoversight/meltzer.htm.

Bibliography

Abbey L., (1990) "Ghana's Experience with Structural Adjustment—Some Lessons," in James Pickett and Hans Singer (eds.), Towards Economic Recovery in Sub-Saharan Africa, Routledge.

Acheampong, I. (1972), Transcript, Acheampong's Statement to the Nation on Ghana's External Debts, February 5, 1972

Adjei Mike (1984), "Death and Pain in Rawlings' Ghana" (London: Black Line Publishing Ltd.)

Afrifa A. (1966), The Ghana Coup, February 24, 1966 (London, Frank Cass)

Ahiakpor, James (1991), "Rawlings, Economic Policy Reform, and the Poor: Consistency or Betrayal?" The Journal of Modern African Studies [Cambridge], 29, No. 4, December 1991, 583–600.

———. (1985) The Success and Failure of Dependency Theory: The Experience of Ghana. International Organization, Summer 535–52.

Akonor, Kwame. (2001), To Fix Ghana's Economy. New York Times. January 10: A18.

Alesina, A., N. Roubini and G. Cohen (1997), Political Cycles and the Macroeconomy, Cambridge MA: MIT Press.

Ames, Barry. (1987), Political Survival: Politicians and Public Policy in Latin America. Berkeley: University of California Press.

Andrzej Krassowski, (1974), Development and the Debt Trap: Economic Planning and External Borrowing in Ghana (London: Overseas Development Institute.

Anin, T. E. (1991), Essays on the Political Economy of Ghana. Accra: Selwyn.

Ankrah, Joseph. (1966), "The Future of the Military in Ghana," Africa Forum [London], 2, No. 1, Summer 1966, 5–16.

Anyemedu K. (1993), "The Economic Policies of the PNDC" in Gyimah-Boadi (ed). Ghana Under PNDC Rule. London: CODESRIA.

Arhin, Kwame (ed.). (1993), The Life and Work of Kwame Nkrumah. Trenton, New Jersey: Africa World Press.

Aryeetey, E. Harrigan and M. Nissanke (editors), (2000), Reforms in Ghana: The Reality and the Mirage, James Currey, Oxford.

——— and A. Cox. (1997), "Aid Effectiveness in Ghana." In Carlsson et al (eds.), Foreign Aid in Africa: Learning from Country Experience, Uppsala: Nordiska Afrika institutet.

Asmah, Kobena Annan. (1986), Ghana's Revolution: The PNDC's Politics of Pragmatic Ideology. (Contemporary National Affairs, Series No. 2) Accra: Kakabaah.

Assimeng, Max (1981), Social Structure of Ghana: A Study in Persistence and Change. Tema: Ghana Publishing Corporation.

———. (1996) An anatomy of modern Ghana, Ghana Academy of Arts and Sciences, Accra, Ghana.

Bandura, A. (1986), Social foundations of thought and action: A social cognitive theory. Englewood Cliffs, NJ: Prentice Hall.

Bank of Ghana. (1985), "Ghana's Stabilisation Measures and the IMF: A Case Study," Africa Development," 10, 1985.

Barker, Peter. (1979), Operation Cold Chop: The Coup That Toppled Nkrumah. (2d ed.) Accra: Ghana Publishing.

Bates, R H, (1988), Toward a Political Economy of Development. A Rational Choice Perspective. Berkeley: University of California Press.

———. (1981), Markets & States in Tropical Africa, University of California Press, Berkeley.

———. (1971), Unions, Parties, and Political Development: a Study of Mineworkers in Zambia, New Haven & London.

Bawumia Mahamuda (1996), The sequencing of fiscal reform during stabilization and structural adjustment: lessons from Ghana, Uganda and Zimbabwe. Comparative Economic Studies; 38: 113–33, Summer–Fall 1996.

Baynham, Simon. (1988), The Military and Politics in Nkrumah's Ghana. Boulder, Colorado: Westview Press.

Beck, Nathaniel. (1982), Does There Exist a Political Business Cycle? A Box-Tiao Analysis. Public Choice 38: 205–v9.

Beckman, Peter C. (1984), World Politics in the 20th Century, Englewood: Prentice Hall-Inc.

Ben-Porath, Y. (1975), "The Years of Plenty and the Years of Famine—A Political Business," Kyklos 28.

Bentsi-Enchill, N.K. (1988), "Year Six of the PNDC: The PNDC and National Policies." West Africa. January 11, 1988.

Biersteker, Thomas (1990), "Reducing the Role of the State in the Economy: A Conceptual Exploration of IMF and World Bank Prescriptions. International Studies Quarterly, 34, no. 4 (December 1990): 477–492.

Birch, Anthony (2001), Concepts & Theories of Modern Democracy. 2nd ed. London: Routledge.

Bird, Graham. (2002), "The Completion Rate of IMF Programmes: What We Know, Don't Know and Need to Know." World Economy 25 (6): 833–847.

———. (1998), "The Effectiveness of Conditionality and the Political Economy of Policy Reforms: Is It Simply a Matter of Political Will?" Journal of Policy Reform (October) 89–113; and Policy Options. International Organization (summer): 477–511.

———. (1996), The International Monetary Fund and Developing Countries: A Review of the Evidence.

———. (1996), "The International Monetary Fund and Developing Countries: A Review of the Evidence and Policy Options." International Organization 50 (3): 477–511.

———. (1996), "Borrowing from the IMF: The Policy Implications of Recent Empirical Research." World Development 24 (11): 1753–1760.

———. (1994), "The Myths and Realities of IMF Lending." World Economy 17 (5): 759–778.

Birmingham, W., I. Neustadt and E.N. Omaboe (eds). (1966), A Study of Contemporary Ghana: Volume 1—The Economy of Ghana, Allen and Unwin, London.

Block S. (2002), "Political Business Cycles, Democratization, and Economic Reform: The Case of Africa," Journal of Development Economics, Vol. 62 205–228. 23).

Boafo-Arthur, K. (2000), "Chieftaincy and the Prospects for Democratic Consolidation in Ghana" Paper presented at a symposium on the theme "Chieftaincy and Development" organized by the Institute of African Studies, University of Ghana, Legon on June 14, 2000.

———. (1999), Structural Adjustment Programs (SAPS) In Ghana: Interrogating PNDC's Implementation, West Africa Review, 15–35.

———. (1999), Ghana: structural adjustment, democratization, and the politics of continuity Kwame Boafo-Arthur. African Studies Review (U.S.); 42, No. 2:41–72, September.

———. (1991), "Prelude to Constitutional Rule: An Assessment of The Process" in Kwame A. Ninsin and Kofi Drah ed. Ghana's transition to Constitutional Rule, Accra: Ghana Universities Press.

Boahen, A. A. (1992), The Ghanaian Sphinx; Reflections on the Contemporary History of Ghana: 1972–1987, Accra, Academy of Arts and Sciences.

———. (1997), "Ghana: Conflict Reoriented" in William Zartman ed. Governance as Conflict Management: Politics and violence in West Africa, Brookings Institution Press

Boorman Jack. (2001), Conditionality in Fund Supported Programs—Policy Issues. Washington DC. IMF.

Boyle, Phelim P. (1984), "Risk Sharing, Incentives and Moral Hazard." in Premium Calculation in Insurance edited by F. de Vylder, M. Goovaerts and J. Haezendonck, 31–75, published by D. Riedel Publishing Company, Dordrecht, Holland.

Bradlow, Daniel. (2001), "Stuffing new wine into old bottles: The troubling case of the IMF." Journal of International Banking Regulation Vol. 3: Number 1 (August 2001) 9–36.

Bretton, Henry L. (1966), The Rise and Fall of Kwame Nkrumah: A Study of Personal Rule in Africa. New York: Praeger, 1966.

Burley, Anne-Marie Slaughter. (1993), "International Law and International Relations Theory: A Dual Agenda." American Journal of International Law 87 (April): 205–39.

Busia, K A. (1966), Africa in Search of Democracy. New York: Praeger.

———. (1956), The present status and aspirations of elites in the Gold Coast. International Social Science Bulletin. 8 (3): 424–431.

Busumtwi-Sam, James (1993), Economic Crisis and Policy Adjustment: The Politics of Foreign Economic Policy Making in Ghana, 1982–1990 Ph.D., University of Toronto.

Callaghy, Thomas M. (1990), "Lost between State and Market: The Politics of Economic Adjustment in Ghana, Zambia and Nigeria," in Joan Nelson ed. Economic Crisis and Policy Choice.

Chand, Sheetal K., and Reinold van Til. (1988), "Ghana: Toward Successful Stabilization and Recovery," Finance and Development, 25, No. 1, March 1988, 32–35.

Chayes, Abram, and Antonia Handler Chayes. (1993), "On Compliance." International Organization 47 (Spring): 175–205.

———. (1995), The New Sovereignty: Compliance with International Regulatory Agreements. Cambridge, MA: Harvard University Press.

Chazan, Naomi. (1994), "Engaging the State: Associational Life in Sub-Saharan Africa." in State Power and Social Forces: Domination and Transformation in the Third World, ed. J. Migdal, A. Kohli, and V. Shue. Cambridge: Cambridge University Press.

———. (1991), "The Political Transformation of Ghana Under the PNDC," in Donald Rothchild ed. Ghana: The Political Economy of Structural Adjustment, Boulder Colorado: Lynne Rienner.

———. (1987), "Ghanaian Politics After 1981: Revolution or Evolution?, Canadian Journal of African Studies , xxi.

——— . (1983), An Anatomy of Ghanaian Politics: Managing Political Recession, 1969–82, Boulder, CO: Westview.

Checkel, Jeffrey. (1998), "The Constructivist Turn in International Relations," World Politics 50 (2).

Cline, William. (1983), "Economic Stabilisation In Developing Countries: Theory and Stylised Facts," in: John Williamson (ed.), IMF Conditionality, Institute for International Economics, Washington, D.C.: 175–208.

Collier, Paul. (1997), "The Failure of Conditionality." In Perspectives on Aid and Development, edited by Catherine Gwin and Joan Nelson. Washington, DC: Overseas Development Council.

Commander Simon, John Howell, and Wayone Seini. (1989), "Ghana: 1983–1987," in Structural Adjustment & Agriculture, ed. Simon Commander (London: Overseas Development Institute).

Corbo, Vittorio and Stanley Fischer. (1995), "Structural Adjustment, Stabilization and Policy Reform: Domestic and International Finance." In Jere Behrman and T.N. Srinivasan, eds. Handbook of Development Economics, Vol. 3B. Amsterdam: Elsevier Science B.V.

Cox, Robert. (1996), "A perspective on Globalization," in James Mittelman, ed., Globalization: Critical Reflections. Boulder: Lynne Rienner Publishers.

———. (1993), "Structural issues of global governance," in S. Gill, ed., Gramsci, historical materialism, and international relations (Cambridge: Cambridge University Press, 1993), pp. 259–89.

Cox, Gary W., and Mathew D. McCubbins. (1986), "Electoral Politics as a Redistributive Game." Journal of Politics 48 (May): 370–89.

Davidson, Basil. (1989), Black Star: A View of the Life and Times of Kwame Nkrumah. Boulder, Colorado: Westview Press.
De Soto, H. (2000), Mystery of Capital: Why Capitalism Triumphs in the West and Fails Everywhere Else, Basic Books.
Decalo, Samuel. (1976), Coups and Army Rule in Africa: Studies in Military Style. New Haven: Yale University Press.
Diabré, Zéphirin. (1999), The Political Economy of Adjustment in Burkina Faso, CAER II Discussion Paper 28, Harvard Institute for International Development.
Diamond, Larry. (1987), Class formation and the swollen African state In: The Journal of Modern African Studies. 25, no. 4 (567–596).
Dick W. (1984), "Authoritarian versus Nonauthoritarian Approaches to Economic Development" Journal of Political Economy (Summer 1994): 817–827.
Dordunoo and V.K. Nyanteng. (1997), "Overview of Ghanaian Economic Development." In V.K. Nyanteng (ed) Policies and Options for Ghanaian Economic Development, Legon: Institute of Statistical, Social and Economic Research, University of Ghana.
Douglas, Evan J. (1989), "The Simple Analytics of the Principal-Agent Incentive Contract." Journal of Economic Education, Winter 1989, 39–51.
Downs, George W., David M. Rocke, and Peter N. Barsoom. (1996), "Is the Good News about Compliance Good News about Cooperation?" International Organization 50 (Summer): 379–406.
Doyle, Michael. (1997), Ways of War and Peace: Realism, Liberalism, and Socialism, New York: W.W. Norton & Company.
Drazen, Allen. (2002), "Conditionality and Ownership in IMF Lending: A Political Economy Approach." IMF Staff Papers 49 (Special Issue): 36–67.
Dreher, A. (2004), Do IMF and IBRD cause moral hazard and political business cycles? Evidence from panel data (with Roland Vaubel), Open Economies Review 15, 1: 5–22.
———. (2003), The Influence of Elections on IMF Programme Interruptions, The Journal of Development Studies 39, 6: 101–120.
———. (2002), "The Development and Implementation of IMF and World Bank Conditionality." HWWA Discussion Paper No. 165. Hamburg: Hamburg Institute of International Economics.
Easterlin, R.A. 91981), "Why Isn't the Whole World Developed?," Journal of Economic History, March 1981.
Economic Intelligent Unit. EIU. (1988), Ghana Country Report, no.3. London.
EIU Country Report: Ghana. London: (2000), The Economist Intelligence Unit.
Edusei Krobo. (1962), "Speech to National Parliament." Parliamentary Debates February 6, 1962
Edwards Sebastian and Guido Tabellini. (1991), Explaining Fiscal Policies and Inflation in Developing Countries. Journal of International Money & Finance 10 (March 1991) p. 16–48.
Edwards, Martin S. (2001a), "Crime and Punishment: Understanding IMF Sanctioning Practices." Working Paper. New Brunswick, NJ: Rutgers University.
———. (2001b), "Sticking with Yes: Domestic Institutions and IMF Compliance." Working Paper.

Etzioni-Halevy, Eva (1997), Classes and Elites in Democracy and Democratization. New York & London: Garland.

Finnemore, Martha. (1996), National Interests in International Society, Cornell University Press.

Fischer, Stanley. (1991), "Macroeconomics, Development, and Growth," NBER Macroeconomics Annual: 29–364.

———. (1987), "Economic Growth and Economic Policy" in Growth-Oriented Adjustment Programs, edited by Vittorio Corbo, Morris Goldstein and Mohsin Khan. Washington, DC: The International Monetary Fund and the World Bank.

Fisiy, F. C. (1995), 'Chieftaincy in the Modern State: An Institution at the Crossroads of Democratic Change' in: Paideuma No. 41 (pp. 49–62).

Fosu, K. (2002), Political Instability and Economic Growth: Implications of Coup Events in Sub-Saharan Africa, The American Journal of Economics And Sociology, Volume 61, January, 2002.

———. (1992), Political instability and economic growth: evidence form sub-Saharan Africa. Economic Development and Cultural change 40 (4), pp. 829–841, 1992.

Frey, B. (1996), Political Business Cycles. Aldershot: Edgar Elgar.

———. and Eichenberger, R. (1994), The political economy of stabilization programmes in developing countries, European Journal of Political Economy 10: 169–190.

Frimpong-Ansah, J.H. (1992), The Vampire State in Africa: The Political Economy of Decline in Ghana, London: James Currey Ltd.

G-7 (2000), 'Statement of G-7 Finance Ministers and Central Bank Governors' (Washington DC, 15 April 2000 LS-556).

Gamarra, Eduardo (1994), "Market-Oriented Reforms and Democratization in Latin America: Challenges of the 1990s," in Latin American Political Economy in the Age of Neoliberal Reform: Theoretical and Comparative Perspectives for the 1990s, eds. William C. Smith, Carlos H. Acuna, and Eduardo A. Gamarra (New Brunswick, NJ: Transaction Publishers).

Garlick, P. (1971), African Traders and Economic Development in Ghana. London: Oxford University Press.

Gayi S. K. (1991), "Adjustment and 'Safety Netting': Ghana's PAMSCAD," Journal of International Development, 3, 5.

Genoud R. (1969), Nationalism and Economic Development in Ghana, New York: Praeger.

Ghana (1964), Ghana Economic Survey, Central Bureau of Statistics, Accra.

———. (1965), Parliamentary Statement by Minister of Finance, September 10, 1965.

———. (1976), Supreme Military Council. Office of the Press Secretary. Fourth Year in Office of Colonel Ignatius Kutu Acheampong, January 13, 1975–January 12, 1976. Accra: Office of the Press Secretary of the SMC, 1976.

———. (1977), General Kutu Acheampong: The Fifth Milestone, January 13, 1976–January 12, 1977. Accra: Office of the Press Secretary of the SMC, 1977.

———. (1986), Economic Recovery Programme 1984–1986, Accra.

———. (1987), National Programme for Economic Development, Revised, Wednesday, July 1, 1987. Accra: 1987.

———. (1987) Programme of Action to Mitigate the Social Costs of Adjustment. Accra: 1987.
Gold, Joseph Gold (1972), Voting and Decisions in the International Monetary Fund (Washington DC: IMF).
Goldstein Judith and Keohane Robert, eds. (1993), Ideas and Foreign Policy (Ithaca, N.Y.: Cornell University Press, 1993): 173–206.
Goldsworthy, David. (1973), "Ghana's Second Republic: A Post Mortem," African Affairs [Oxford], 72, No. 286, 1973, 8–25.
Gonzalez, M. (1999), "On Elections, Democracy and Macroeconomic Policy Cycles," working paper, Department of Economics, Princeton University.
Graham, Y. (1989), "From GTP to Assene: Aspects of Industrial Working Class Struggles in Ghana, 1982–1989," in Emmanuel Hansen and Kwame A. Ninsin, eds., The State, Development and Politics in Ghana. London: Cordesria.
———. (1985), The Politics of Crisis in Ghana: Class Struggle and Organization, 1981–84 Review of African Political Economy, Vol. 12 No. 34 (Winter 1985), pp. 54–68
Green Daniel (1995), Ghana's 'Adjusted' Democracy, Review of African Political Economy—Vol. 22 No. 66, (December 1995).
Green, R.H. (1987), Stabilization and Adjustment Programmes and Policies: Ghana, World Institute for Development Economic Research, Helsinki.
Grier, K. (1989), "On the Existence of a Political Monetary Cycle," American Journal of Political Science 33, 376–89.
Grossman, S., and Hark O. (1983), "An Analysis of the Principal Agent Problem." Econometrica, January, 51, 7–45.
Guillaumont, S. Guillaumont and J. F. Brun. (1999), How Instability Lowers African Growth, Journal of African Economies 8(1), pp 87–107.
Guitian, Manuel. (1981), Fund Conditionality: Evolution of Principles and Practices. Washington, DC: International Monetary Fund.
Gupta, Sanjeev, Jerald Schiff, and Benedict Clements. (1996), "Worldwide Military Spending, 1990–95," IMF Working Paper 96/64 (Washington: International Monetary Fund).
Gyekye Kwame (1996), African Cultural Values: An Introduction, Accra, Ghana: Sankofa Publishing.
Gyimah-Boadi, E. (1994), "Associational Life, Civil Society, and Democratization in Ghana." Pp. 125–148 in Civil Society and the State in Africa, ed. J. Harbeson, D. Rothchild, and N. Chazan. Boulder, CO: Lynne Reiner.
———. (ed.). (1993), Ghana Under PNDC Rule, 1982–1989. Dakar: Codesria
———. (1991), "Tensions in Ghana's Transition to Constitutional Rule" in Kwame A. Ninsin and Kofi Drah ed. Ghana's Transition to Constitutional Rule, Accra: Ghana Universities Press.
———. "Ghana," in Paul Mosley, Jane Harrigan and John Toye (eds) (1991), Aid and Power: the World Bank and Policy-based Lending. Volume 2: Case Studies, London and New York: Routledge.
———. (1990), "Economic Recovery and Politics in PNDC's Ghana," The Journal of Commonwealth and Comparative Politics, vol. xxviii, no. 3.

Haas, Peter M. (1998), "Compliance with EU Directives: Insights from International Relations and Comparative Politics," in: Journal of European Policy, 5(1), March 1998, 17–37.

Haggard, Stephan and Robert R. Kaufman. (1995), The Political Economy of Democratic Transitions (Princeton: Princeton University Press).

———. and S. B. Webb (eds.). (1994), Voting for Reform: Democracy, Political Liberalization, and Economic Adjustment, New York: Oxford University Press.

———. (1985), "The Politics of Adjustment: Lessons from the IMF's Extended Fund Facility," International Organization, Vol. 39, no. 3 (Summer).

———. (1985), The Politics of Stabilization: Lessons from the IMF's Extended Fund Facility, "International Organization 39, 3 (Summer 1985); reprinted in Miles Kahler, ed., The Politics of International Debt (Ithaca: Cornell University Press, 1986).

———. and Robert R. Kaufman (1989), "Economic Adjustment in New Democracies" in Fragile Coalitions: The Politics of Economic Adjustment, Transaction Books, New Brunswick (USA).

———. Jean-Dominique Lafay and Christian Morrisson. (1995), Political Feasibility of Adjustment in Developing Countries. Paris: OECD Development Centre.

Hansen, E. (1991), Ghana Under Rawlings: Early Years, Lagos: Malthouse Press Limited.

——— and Kwame A. Ninsin (eds.). (1989), The State, Development, and Politics in Ghana. London: Codesria.

——— . (1987), "The State and Popular Struggles in Ghana, 1982–1986" in Peter Anyang' Nyong'o ed. Popular Struggles for Democracy in Africa, London: Zed.

Hapggod David. (1965), Africa: From Independence to Tomorrow, NY: Atheneum.

Harvey, Charles. (1991), "Recovery from Macroeconomic Disaster in Sub-Saharan Africa," unpublished manuscript.

Haynes, Jeff. (1991), "Human Rights and Democracy in Ghana: The Record of the Rawlings' Regime," African Affairs [Oxford], 90, No. 360, July 1991, 407–25.

Heckelman, J. and Berument, H. (1998), Political business cycles and endogenous elections, Southern Economic Journal, 64, 987–1000.

Henkin, Louis. (1979), How Nations Behave: Law and Foreign Policy. New York: Council on Foreign Relations. McCallum, Bennett T. 1978. The Political Business Cycle: An Empirical Test. Southern Economic Journal 44: 504–15.

Herbst, J. (1993), The Politics of Reform In Ghana, 1982–1991, Berkeley, CA: University of California Press.

———. (1990), "The Structural Adjustment of Politics in Africa," World Development 18: 949–958.

Hopkins, R., A. Powell, A. Roy and C.L. Gilbert. (1997), "'The World Bank and conditionality.'" Journal of International Development, 9(4); June.

Horsefield, Keith J. (1996), The International Monetary Fund, 1945–1965: Twenty Years of International Monetary Cooperation, Vol. 1 (Washington D.C., IMF, 1996).

Howard, Rhoda. (1978), Colonialism and Underdevelopment in Ghana. New York: Africana.

Huq, M. M. (1989), The Economy of Ghana: The First 25 Years Since Independence. New York: St. Martin's Press.
Hurd, Ian. (1999), Legitimacy and authority in international politics. International Organization. Spring. Vol. 53, 379–408.
Hussain, I. and R. Faruquee (eds) (1994), Adjustment in Africa: Lessons from Country Case Studies, World Bank Regional and Sectoral Studies, Washington, DC: World Bank.
Hutchcroft, P. D. (1997), "The Politics of Privilege: Assessing the Impacts of Rent, Corruption, and Clientelism on Third World Development," in P Heywood, ed, Political Corruption, Oxford: Blackwell & The Political Studies Association, pp. 223–242.
Hutchful Eboe. (2002), Ghana's Adjustment Experience: The Paradox of Reform. Heinemann. Portsmouth, NH.
———. (1997), "Military Policy and Reform in Ghana," The Journal of Modern African Studies, 35, 2.
———. (1987), The IMF and Ghana: The Confidential Record. London: Institute for African Alternatives.
———. (1985), "IMF Adjustment Policies in Ghana since 1966," Africa Development, vol. x , no. ½
IFIAC (International Financial Institution Advisory Commission or Meltzer Commission Report). (2000), Final Report and transcripts of meetings and hearings (Washington DC): http://www.bicusa.org/usgovtoversight/meltzer.htm.
IMF. (2003), Structural Conditionality in Fund-Supported Programs, February 16, http://www.imf.org.
———. (2002), International Financial Statistics CD-ROM, Washington, D.C.
———. (2001), Review of Experience with Evaluation in the Fund (Prepared by the Evaluation Group of Executive Directors). Washington DC: IMF.
———. (2001), Strengthening Country Ownership of Fund-Supported Programs (Washington DC, IMF, December 14, 2001).
———. Occasional Paper No. 199 (2001), Ghana: Economic Development in a Democratic Environment, by Pellechio, Anthony; Zanforlin, Luisa; Begashaw, Girma; Fabrizio, Stefania; and Harnack, Joachim, Washington DC, January 4, 2001.
———. (2001), Ghana: 2001 Article IV Consultation and Third Review under the Poverty Reduction and Growth Facility and Request for Waiver of Performance Criteria, IMF Country Report No. 01/141, August 9, 2001.
———. (2001), Memorandum of Economic and Financial Policies of the Government of Ghana for 2001 (June 11 2001). Washington DC. IMF Publications.
———. (2000), Report to the IMF Executive Board of the Quota Formula Review Group (Washington DC, IMF, 28 April, 2000).
———. (1999), "External Evaluation of IMF Surveillance." Report by a Group of Independent Experts (Washington DC; IMF, 1999).
———. (1999), Poverty Reduction Strategy Papers—Operational Issues, Washington DC, December 10, 1999.
———. (1997), Reducing Unproductive Expenditures is Important for Fiscal Adjustment, IMF Survey 49–51.

———. (1991), Ghana: Adjustment and Growth, 1983–1991. Washington DC. IMF Publications.

Jadhav, Narendra (2000), 'IMF Quota Formulas and Mechanisms: A Developing Economy Perspective' (prepared for G-24 Technical Group Meeting, Lima 1 March 2000).

Jeffries, Richard. (1982), "Rawlings and the Political Economy of Underdevelopment in Ghana," African Affairs [Oxford], 81, No. 324, July 1982, 307–17.

Jeong, Ho-Won. (1995), Liberal economic reform in Ghana: a contested political agenda, Africa Today v. 42 no. 4.

Jonah Kwesi. (1989). "The Social Impact of Ghana's Adjustment Program, 1983-86," in Bade Onimode ed. The IMF, the World Bank and the African Debt, vol. 2: The Social and Political Impact, London: Zed.

Ka, Samba, and Nicolas van de Walle. (1994), "Senegal: Stalled Reform in a Dominant Party System." In Stephan Haggard and Steven B. Webb, ed. Voting for Reform. New York: Oxford University Press, 290–359.

Kahler, Miles. (2001), Leadership Selection in the Major Multilaterals (Washington DC: Institute of International Economics).

Kanbur, S.M. Ravi. 1987. "Structural Adjustment, Macroeconomic Adjustment and Poverty: A Methodology for Analysis." World Development, 15: 1515–1526.

Kapur Devesh and Webb Richard. (2000), Governance-Related Conditionalities of the International Financial Institutions. UNCTAD G-24 Discussion Paper No. 6. New York. United Nations Publications.

———. (2000), "Who Gets to Run the World?," Foreign Policy, No. 121, November/December 2000: pp. 44–50).

Kapur, Ishan ; Hadjimichael, Michael T; Hilbers, Paul; Schiff, Jerald; and Szymczak, Philippe (1991), "Ghana: Adjustment and Growth, 1983–91" IMF Series: Occasional Paper, No. 86, March 15, 1991.

Keohane Robert. (1984), After Hegemony: Cooperation and Discord in the World Political Economy. Princeton: Princeton University Press.

———. and Joseph S. Nye. (1989), Power and Interdependence, Harper Collins, New York.

———. ed. 1986. Neorealism and Its Critics. New York: Columbia University Press.

———. and Lisa Martin. (1995), "The Promise of Institutionalist Theory." International Security 20 (Summer): 39–51.

———. (1988), "International Institutions: Two Approaches," International Studies Quarterly, vol. 32, no. 4 (December): 379–396.

Khan Mohsin. (1990), "The Macroeconomic Effects of Fund-Supported Adjustment Programs," IMF Staff Papers 37, no. 2.

Killick, T. with Ramani Gunatilaka and Ana Marr. (1998), Aid and the Political Economy of Policy Change, London: Routledge/ODI.

———. (1993), The Adaptive Economy: Adjustment Policies in Small, Low-income Countries. Washington, D.C.: World Bank, 1993.

———. (1998), Aid and the Political Economy of Policy Change (London: Overseas Development Institute).

———. (1997), 'Principals, agents and the failings of conditionality.' Journal of International Development, 9(4) June.

———. (1995), IMF Programmes in Developing Countries: Design and Impact. London and New York: Routledge and Overseas Development Institute.
———. (1983), Kenya, the IMF, and the Unsuccessful Quest for Stabilization, in: John Williamson (ed.), IMF Conditionality, Institute for International Economics, Washington, D.C.: 381–414.
———. (1978), Development Economics in Action: A Study of Economic Policies in Ghana, New York: St. Martin's Press.
Kofi, Tetteh A. (1994), Structural adjustment in Africa: a performance review of World Bank policies under uncertainty in commodity price trends, UNU World Institute for Development Economics Research (UNU/WIDER): Helsinki : WIDER.
Krafona, Kwesi (ed.). (1988), Organization of African Unity: 25 Years On: Essays in Honor of Kwame Nkrumah. London: Afroworld.
Kramer, Gerald H. (1983), "The Ecological Fallacy Revisited: Aggregate- versus Individual-level Findings on Economics and Elections, and Sociotropic Voting." American Political Science Review 77(1): 92–111.
Krasner, Stephen D. (1983), International Regimes. Ithaca: Cornell University Press.
Kraus, Jon. (2002), "Capital, Power and Business Associations in The African Political Economy: A Tale Of Two Countries, Ghana and Nigeria." The Journal of Modern African Studies vol. 40, no. 3: 395–436.
———. (1987), "Ghana's Shift from Radical Populism," Current History, 86, No. 520, May 1987, 205–08, 227–28.
Krueger, A. and I. Turan (1993), "The Politics and Economics of Turkish Policy Reform in the 1980's" Bates and A. Krueger, eds. (1993), Political and Economic Interactions in Economic Policy Reform: Evidence from Eight Countries, Oxford: Basil Blackwell.
———. (1993), Political Economy of Policy Reform in Developing Countries. Cambridge: MIT.
———. M. Schiff, and A. Valdes. (1988), "Measuring the Effect of Sectoral and Economy wide Policies." World Bank Economic Review, 2: 255–271.
Kuznets, S. (1966), Modern Economic Growth: Rate, Structure, and Spread, Yale University Press, New Haven, 1966.
Laguerre, Michel S. (1993), The Military and Society in Haiti. Knoxville: University of Tennessee Press, TN.
Lal, D. (1983), The Poverty of Development Economics. Hobart Paperbacks 16. London: Institute of Economic Affairs.
Leechor, C. (1994) "Ghana: Frontrunner in Adjustment," in Ishrat Husain and Rashid Faruque (eds) Adjustment in Africa: Lessons from Case Studies. DC: World Bank.
Leite, Sergio Pereira and Pellechio, Anthony. (2000), Ghana: Economic Development in a Democratic Environment. Washington: IMF, 2000. (Occasional Paper).
Leith, J. Clark and M. Lofchie (1993), "The Political Economy of Structural Adjustment in Ghana, in Bates, R. H. and A. O. Krueger, eds, Political and Economic Interactions in Economic Policy Reform: Evidence from Eight Countries. Cambridge, MA: Blackwell: 225–293.

———. (1974), Foreign Trade Regimes and Economic Development: Ghana, Columbia University Press, New York.

LeVine, Victor T. (1975), Political Corruption: The Ghana Case. Stanford: Hoover Institution Press.

Lewis, W.A. (1953), Report on the Industrialisation of the Gold Coast, Government of Ghana, Accra.

Lewis-Beck, Michael S. (1988), Economics and Elections. Ann Arbour, Michigan: University of Michigan Press.

Libby, Roland L. (1976), "External Co-optation of a Less Developed Country's Policy Making: The Case of Ghana, 1969–1972," World Politics, vol. xxix, no. 1

Limann, Hilla. (1980), Limann Speaks: "The Way Ahead." Address by His Excellency President Hilla Limann at the Annual Congress of the People's National Party (May 29 to June 1, 1980) at the Prempeh Assembly.

Lipson, Charles. (1991), "Why Are Some International Agreements Informal?" International Organization 45 (Autumn): 495–538.

Loxley, J. (1988), Ghana: Economic Crisis and the Long Road to Recovery, The North-South Institute, Ottawa.

Ludger, Schuknecht. (1996), Political Business Cycles and Fiscal Policies in Developing Countries, Kyklos, Vol. 49 #2, pp. 155–170.

Mann, Michael. (1993). The sources of social power: Volume ll. New York: Cambridge University Press.

March, J.G. and J.P. Olsen. (1998), The institutional dynamics of international political orders. International Organization 52 (4): 943–969. Keohane and S.D. Krasner (eds.) 1999, Exploration and Contestation in the Study of World Politics: 303–329. Cambridge, MA: The MIT Press.

Markovitz I. L. (2002). "Civil Society, Pluralism, Goldilocks, and other Fairy Tales in Africa," pp. 117–145 in Contested Terrains and Constructed Categories: Contemporary Africa in Focus, eds., George Bond and Nigel Gibson, Boulder, CO.: Westview Press.

———. (1998), "Uncivil Society, the State, and Capitalism in Africa," pp. 21–53 in Civil Society in Africa?, Nelson Kasfir, ed., London: Frank Cass.

———. (1987) (ed.), Studies in Power and Class in Africa (New York: Oxford University Press

———. (1977) Power and Class in Africa, Englewood Cliffs: Prentice Hall

Markus, Gregory B. (1988), "The Impact of Personal and National Economic Conditions on the Presidential Vote: A Pooled Cross-Sectional Analysis." American Journal of Political Science 32(1):137–154.

Marshall, C. & Rossman, G.B. (1989), Designing Qualitative Research, Newbury Park, California: Sage.

Martin, Lisa and Simmons Beth. (1998), "Theories and Empirical Studies of International Institutions" International Organization 52 (Autumn): 729—757.

———. (1993), "Credibility, Costs, and Institutions: Cooperation on Economic Sanctions." World Politics 45 (April): 406–32.

———. (1992), Coercive Cooperation: Explaining Multilateral Economic Sanctions. Princeton, N.J.: Princeton University Press.

Masten, J and Brown S. (1995), Problems facing business associations in emerging countries: The case of Ghana, International Small Business Journal, July-September, Vol. 13, No. 4. pp. 91–96.

Matthew, Martin. (1991), "Negotiating Adjustment and External Finance: Ghana and the International Community, 1982–1989," in Donald Rothchild ed. Ghana: The Political Economy of Structural Adjustment, Boulder, Colorado: Lynne Rienner.

Mayer, Wolfgang and Alex Mourmouras. (2002), "Vested Interests in a Political Theory of IFI Conditionality." IMF Working Paper No. 02/73. Washington, DC: IMF.

McCallum, Bennett T. (1978), The Political Business Cycle: An Empirical Test. Southern Economic Journal 44: 504–15.

McGowan, P. and Johnson, T. (1984), "African Military Coups d'Etat and Underdevelopment: A Quantitative Historical Analysis," The Journal of Modern African Studies, 22: 633–666.

McRae, D. (1977), "A Political Model of the Business Cycle," Journal of Political Economy 85, 239–63.

Mearsheimer, John. (1994–95), "The False Promise of International Institutions." International Security 19 (Winter): 5–26.

———. (1990), "Back to the Future: Instability in Europe after the Cold War," International Security 15: 5–57.

Mecagni, Mauro. (1999), "The Causes of Program Interruptions," in H. Bredenkamp, S. Schadler (eds.), Economic Adjustment in Low-Income Countries, International Monetary Fund, Washington, D.C.: 215–276.

Meisel, James (1958), The Myth of the Ruling Class. Gaetano Mosca and the "Elite." Ann Arbor: University of Michigan Press.

Migdal, J.S. Atul Kohli and Vivienne Shue (eds.) (1994), State Power and Social Forces. New York: Cambridge University Press.

———. (1988) Strong Societies and Weak States. Princeton: Princeton University Press.

———. (1987), Strong States, Weak States: Power and Accommodation. In M. Weiner & M. Huntington (eds.). Understanding Political Development. New York: HarperCollins Publishers. 391–436.

Mills, C. Wright. (1956), The Power Elite. New York: Oxford University Press.

Monroe Kristen Renwick ed., (1991), The Economic Approach to Politics: A Critical Reassessment of the Theory of Rational Action. New York: HarperCollins.

Morrison, Donald G. and Hugh Michael Stevenson. (1971), "Political instability in independent Black Africa: More dimensions within nations." Journal of Conflict Resolution 15 (September), 347–368.

Mosca, Gaetano. (1939), The Ruling Class. New York & London: McGraw-Hill.

Mosley, Paul (ed.) Jane Harrigan and John Toye (1998), Aid and Power: The World Bank and Policy-based Lending, Volume 2. London: Routledge.

———. Jane Harrigan and John Toye (1995), Aid and Power: The World Bank and Policy-based Lending, Volume 1. London: Routledge, 2nd edition.

———. (1992), Development Finance and Policy Reform: Essays in the Theory and Practice of Conditionality in Less Developed Countries, New York: St. Martin's Press.

Nafziger, E. W. (1993), The Debt Crisis in Africa, Baltimore: Johns Hopkins University Press.
———. (1988), Inequality in Africa: Political Elites, Proletariat, Peasants, and the Poor. Cambridge: Cambridge University Press.
Nelson Joan, ed., (1996), "Promoting Policy Reforms: The Twilight of Conditionality?" World Development 24: 1551–1559.
———. and Stephanie J. Eglinton. (1993), Global Goals, Contentious Means: Issues of Multiple Aid Conditionality. Washington, DC: Overseas Development Council.
———. (1992), "Poverty, Equity, and the Politics of Adjustment." In The Politics of Economic Adjustment, ed. Stephan Haggard and Robert R. Kauffman. Princeton, NJ: Princeton University Press. Pp. 221- 69.
———. (1990) "Introduction: The Politics of Economic Adjustment in Developing Nations" in Economic Crisis and Policy Choice. The Politics of Adjustment in the Third World. Edited by Joan M. Nelson, (Princeton University Press, Princeton, New Jersey).
———. (1990). Economic Crisis and Policy Choice: The Politics of Adjustment in the Third World (Princeton: Princeton University Press).
Nikoi Kote-Nikoi. (1996), Beyond the New Orthodoxy: Africa's Debt and Development Crisis in Retrospect Ashgate Publishing.
Ninsin K. (ed.), (1998), Ghana: Transition to Democracy, Dakar: CODESRIA.
———. (1991), The informal sector in Ghana's political economy, Freedom Publication, Accra, Ghana
———. (1991). "The Impact of the PNDC's Economic Reform Policies on Ghanaian Society and Politics, 1983–88" in Legon Journal of Humanities, vol. 5.
———. (1991). "The PNDC and the Problem of Legitimacy" in Donald Rothchild ed. Ghana: The Political Economy of Structural Adjustment, Boulder, Colorado: Lynne Rienner.
———. (1989), "State, Capital and Labor Relations, 1961–1987" in E. Hansen and K. A. Ninsin ed. The State, Development and Politics in Ghana, London: CODESRIA.
———. (1987), "Ghanaian Politics After 1981: Revolution or Evolution?" Canadian Journal of African Studies [Ottawa], 21, No. 1, 1987, 17–37.
Nkrumah, Kwame. (1968), Dark Days in Ghana. London: Lawrence and Wishart.
———. (1963), Africa Must Unite. New York: Praeger.
———. (1965), Neo-Colonialism: The Last Stage of Imperialism. London: Nelson.
———. (1961), I Speak of Freedom: A Statement of African Ideology. London: Heinemann.
Nordhaus, W. (1975), The Political Business Cycle, Review of Economic Studies 42: 169–190.
———. (1989), Alternative Models to Political Business Cycles, Brookings Papers on Economic Activity, The Brookings Institution, 2: 1–50.
Nowak, M. et al. (1996), "Ghana, 1983–1991." In Hadjimichael, M. T. and others Adjustment for Growth: The African Experience, IMF Occasional Working Paper No. 143, Washington DC: IMF.
Nugent, P. (1995), Big Men, Small Boys and Politics in Ghana, Accra: Asempa Publishers.

Nyanteng, V.K. (1997), Policies and Options for Ghanaian Economic Development, Legon: Institute of Statistical, Social and Economic Research, University of Ghana.
Ocran, Albert Kwesi. (1968), A Myth Is Broken: An Account of the Ghana Coup d'Etat of 24th February 1966. New York: Humanities Press.
Oelbaum, Jay. (2002), "Populist Reform Coalitions in Sub-Saharan Africa : Ghana's Triple Alliance" Canadian Journal of African Studies vol. 36, no. 2:281–328.
Ofuatey Kodjoe. (1998) "Ideology and Public Policy in Ghana" in Mengusteab K. and Adams F. Globalization and the dilemmas of the South. Boulder. London, Macmillan.
———. (1985) "Elites and Foreign Policy: A Political Economy Approach: The case of Ghana, 1972–1978 (unpublished).
Ofusu-Appiah, L.H. (1972), The Life of Lt. Gen. E.K. Kotoka. Accra: Waterville Publishing.
Olson, Mancur. (1982), The Rise and Decline of Nations. New Haven, CT: Yale University Press.
Omari, T. Peter. (1970), Kwame Nkrumah: Anatomy of an African Dictatorship. New York: Africana.
Oquaye M. A. (1980), Politics in Ghana, 1972–1979, Accra: Tornado Publishers.
Ould-Mey Mohameden. (1994), "Global Adjustments: Implications for Peripheral States," Third World Quarterly 15(2): 319–336.
Owusu, Maxwell. (1972), "The Search for Solvency: Background to the Fall of Ghana's Second Republic, 1969–1972," Africa Today, 19, No. 1, 52–60.
———. (19710, "Ghana: What Went Wrong, A Response," Africa Today, 19, No. 2, 1972, 77–80.
Owusu-Ansah, David, and Daniel M. McFarland. (1995), Historical Dictionary of Ghana. Metuchen, New Jersey: Scarecrow Press.
Oye, Kenneth. (1986), Explaining Cooperation Under Anarchy: Hypotheses and Strategies, Princeton: Princeton University Press.
Paldam, M. (1979), "Is There an Electoral Cycle? A Comparative Study of National Accounts," Scandinavian Journal of Economics 81, 323–42.
Panford, K. (1997), "Ghana: A Decade of IMF/World Bank's Policies of Adjustment (1985–1995)," Scandinavian Journal of Development Alternatives and Area Studies, vol. 16, no. 2.
Parry, Geraint. (1969), Political Elites. London: Allen & Unwin.
Persson T. and G. Tabellini (1990). Macroeconomic Policy, Credibility and Politics. Chur: Harwood Academic Publishers.
Picciotto S. (1991), "The internationalization of the state," Capital & Class 43, Spring 1991, pp. 43–63.
Pickney, Robert. (1972), Ghana under Military Rule: 1966–1969. London: Methuen.
———. (1970), Ghana Under Military Rule: 1966–1969, London: Methuen and Co. Ltd.
Plaut, Steven E. and Arie L. Melnik. (2003), "International Institutional Lending Agreements to Sovereign Borrowers." Journal of International Money and Finance. 22 (4): 459–481.

Polak, Jacques J. (1991), The Changing Nature of IMF Conditionality. Essay in International Finance No. 184. Princeton, NJ: Princeton University.

Price, Robert M. (1984), "Neo-colonialism and Ghana's Economic Decline: A Critical Assessment," Canadian Journal of African Studies [Ottawa], 18, No. 1, 163–94.

Przeworski, Adam. (1992). "The Neoliberal Fallacy" Journal of Democracy vol. 3, No. 3 July.

———. (1991), Democracy and the Market: Political and Economic Reforms in Eastern Europe and Latin America (New York: Cambridge University Press).

Putnam, Robert D. (1976), The Comparative Study of Elites. Englewood Cliffs, NJ: Prentice Hall.

Ray, Donald. (1986), Ghana: Politics, Economics and Society. Boulder, Colorado: Lynne Rienner.

Remmer, Karen. (1998) The Politics of Neoliberal Economic Reform in South America, 1980–1994, Studies in Comparative International Development, Summer 1998, Vol. 33, No. 2 pp. 3–29.

———. (1993). The Political Economy of Elections in Latin America, 1980–1991. American Political Science Review 87 (2): 393–407.

———. (1986), The politics of economic stabilization: IMF standby programs in Latin America, 1954–1984, Comparative Politics, Vol. 9, 1: 1–24.

Riddel Barry, (1992). "Things Fall Apart Again: Structural Adjustment Programs in Sub- Saharan Africa" Journal of Modern African Studies, 30, 1.

Rimmer, Douglas. (1992), Staying Poor: Ghana's Political Economy, 1950–1990. New York: Pergamon.

Rodney, Walter. (1982), How Europe Underdeveloped Africa. Washington: Howard University Press.

Rodrik, Dani. (1996), "Understanding economic policy reform." Journal of Economic Literature, XXXIV; March.

Rogoff, K. and A. Sibert. (1988), "Elections and Macroeconomic Policy Cycles," Review of Economic Studies 55, 1–16.

Rose, A. M., (1954), Theory and Method in the Social Sciences, University of Minnesota Press.

Rothchild, D. (ed.) 1991. The Political Economy of Recovery, SAIS African Studies Library, Boulder and London: Lynne Rienner.

Ruggie, John Gerard. (1992), "Multilateralism: The Anatomy of an Institution," International Organization 46, no. 3 (Summer): 561–98.

Rummel Rudolph. (1976), Understanding Conflict and War. Beverly Hills, California: Sage Publications.

Santiso, Carlos. (2001), Good Governance and Aid Conditionality: the World Bank and Conditionality. Georgetown Public Policy Review, Fall 2001: 1–22, vol. 7 #1.

Sappington, David E. M. (1991), "Incentives in Principal-Agent Relationships." Journal of Economic Perspectives 5 (Spring): 45–66.

Schady, Nobert. (2000), The Political Economy of Expenditures by the Peruvian Social Fund Foncodes, 1991–95. American Political Science Review. June 2000.

Schneider, Friedrich, and Bruno S. Frey. (1988), Politico-economic Models of Macroeconomic Policy: A Review of the Empirical Evidence. In Political Business

Cycles. The Political Economy of Money, Inflation and Unemployment, edited by D. Willet. Durham and London: Duke University Press.
Schuknecht, Ludger (1999), Fiscal Policy Cycles and the Exchange Rate Regime in Developing Countries. European Journal of Political Economy 15: 569–80.
———. (1996), "Political Business Cycles and Fiscal Policies in Developing Countries," Kyklos, Vol. 49, 2: 155–170.
Selznick, Philip. (1966), TVA and the Grass-Roots. New York: Harper and Row.
Shepsle K., B. Weingast, and P. Johnson. (1981), "The Political Economy of Costs and Benefits." Journal of Political Economy.
Shillington, Kevin. (1992), Ghana and the Rawlings Factor. New York: St. Martin's Press.
Simmons, Beth A. (1998), "Compliance with International Agreements." Annual Review of Political Science 1: 75–93.
Sklar, R (1979), The Nature of Class Domination In Africa, Journal of Modern African Studies, December 1979, 531–552.
Snidal, Duncan. (1996), "International Political Economy Approaches to International Institutions," International Review of Law and Economics 16, no. 1 (March): 121–37.
Stallings, Barbara. (1992), "International Influence on Economic Policy: Debt, Stabilization, and Structural Reform." In Stephan Haggard and Robert Kaufman, eds., The Politics of Economic Adjustment: International Constraints, Distributive Politics, and the State. Princeton University Press.
Steel, W.F., & Webster, L.M. (1992), How Small Enterprises in Ghana Have Responded to Adjustment. The World Bank Economic Review, 6, 423–438.
Stepan, Alfred. (1990), "On the Tasks of a Democratic Opposition" Journal of Democracy vol. 1, no. 2 Spring.
Stockwell, John. (1978), In Search of Enemies, London, Futura.
Stone, Randall W. (2002), Lending Credibility: The International Monetary Fund and the Post-Communist Transition. Princeton, NJ: Princeton University Press.
Szerezewski, R. (1965), Structural Changes in the Economy of Ghana, Weidenfeld and Nicolson, London.
Tait, Alan. (1990), "IMF Advice on Fiscal Policy," Finance and Development (Washington), Vol. 27 (March 1990), pp. 3336.
Tangri, R. (1992), "The Politics of Government-Business Relations in Ghana." Journal of Modern African Studies vol. 30, no. 1, pp. 97–111.
Thompson, Willard S. (1969), Ghana's Foreign Policy, 1957–1966: Diplomacy, Ideology, and the New State. Princeton: Princeton University Press.
Toye, J. "Ghana's Economic Reforms, 1983–87: Origins, Achievements and Limitations," in James Pickett and H. Singer (eds) 1990. Towards Economic Recovery in Sub-Saharan Africa: Essays in Honor of Robert Gardiner, London and New York, Routledge.
Trades Union Congress (1988) "Economic Survey of Ghana, 1980–1987," Accra.
Tsikata T. (1990), Ghana, in A. Adedeji, S. Rasheed and M. Morrison, eds., The Human Dimensions of Africa's Persistent Crisis. London: Hans Zell.
Tsikata Yvonne M. (1999), "Aid and Reform in Ghana," in Shanta Devarajan; Dollar, D.; Holmgren, T. / World Bank.

Tufte, E. (1978), Political Control of the Economy. Princeton: Princeton University Press.

Vaubel, Roland. (1983), "The Moral Hazard of IMF Lending." World Economy 6 (3): 291–303.

Waldner, David. (1999), State Building and Late Development, Cornell Univ. Press.

Waltz, Kenneth N. (1979), Theory of International Politics, Addison-Wesley, London.

Warnier, J. P., (1993), "The King as a Container in the Cameroon Grassfields" in: Paideuma No. 39 (pp. 303–319).

Weiss, Edith Brown, and Harold K. Jacobson, eds. (1998), Engaging Countries: Strengthening Compliance with International Accords. Cambridge, MA: MIT Press.

Wendt, Alexander. (1992), "Anarchy is What States Make of It: The Social Construction of State Politics," International Organization 46, no. 2 (Spring): 391–425.

Wildavsky A. (1987), The Art and Craft of Policy Analysis, New Brunswick, NJ: Transaction Books. First edition: 1979.

Wilkin, Sam, H. Brandon Haller Helmut Norpoth. (1997), "From Argentina to Zambia: A World-wide Test of Economic Voting." Electoral Studies 16: 301–316.

Williamson, John. (1993), Democracy and the 'Washington Consensus.' World Development, 21 (8), 1329–1336.

Wintrobe, Ronald. (1998), The Political Economy of Dictatorship. Cambridge: Cambridge University Press.

World Bank. (1995), Adjustment in Africa: Reforms, Results, and the Road Ahead. Washington, DC: World Bank.

———. (1991), Ghana, Progress on Adjustment, Report No. 9475-GH. World Bank, Washington, DC.

———. (1990), Ghana: Moving Toward Sustainable Private Sector Led Growth, Western African Department. World Bank, Washington, DC.

Yeebo, Z. (1991), Ghana: The Struggle for Popular Power. Rawlings: Saviour or Demagogue, London: New Beacon Press.

Young, Crawford. (1982), Ideology and Development in Africa. New Haven: Yale University Press.

Young, Oran. (1994), International Governance: Protecting the Environment in a Stateless Society. Ithaca: Cornell University Press.

Younger, S. (19920, "Aid and the Dutch Disease: Macroeconomic Management When Everybody Loves You," World Development 20 (11), November.

Ziorklui, Emmanuel Doe. (1988), Ghana: Nkrumah to Rawlings. Accra: Em-zed Books Centre.

Zulu, Justin B., Nsouli, Saleh M. (1985), Adjustment Programs in Africa: The Recent Experience, IMF Occasional Papers 34, Washington, D.C. http://www.imf.org.

Index

H

I

M

N

For Product Safety Concerns and Information please contact our EU
representative GPSR@taylorandfrancis.com
Taylor & Francis Verlag GmbH, Kaufingerstraße 24, 80331 München, Germany

www.ingramcontent.com/pod-product-compliance
Ingram Content Group UK Ltd.
Pitfield, Milton Keynes, MK11 3LW, UK
UKHW022120190926
475702UK00013B/1558
9780415653473